WITHDRAWN
UTSA LIBRARIES

Finding the Priority Path
Overcoming Organizational Obstacles

Bryant L. Stringham, Ph.D.
Jon D. Stephens

INTERLINK
PUBLICATIONS

Finding the Priority Path: Overcoming Organizational Obstacles
Bryant L. Stringham, Ph.D. and Jon D. Stephens

COPYRIGHT © 2005 by Texere, an imprint of Thomson/South-Western, a part of The Thomson Corporation. Thomson and the Star logo are trademarks used herein under license.

Composed by: Interactive Composition Corporation

Printed in the United States of America by: RR Donnelley, Crawfordsville

1 2 3 4 5 08 07 06 05
This book is printed on acid-free paper.

ISBN 0-324-31219-9

This publication is designed to provide accurate and authoritative information in regard to the subject matter covered. It is sold with the understanding that the publisher is not engaged in rendering legal, accounting, or other professional services. If expert assistance is required, the services of a competent professional person should be sought.

ALL RIGHTS RESERVED.

No part of this work covered by the copyright hereon may be reproduced or used in any form or by any means—graphic, electronic, or mechanical, including photocopying, recording, taping, Web distribution, or information storage and retrieval systems, or in any other manner—without the written permission of the publisher.

The names of all companies or products mentioned herein are used for identification purposes only and may be trademarks or registered trademarks of their respective owners. Texere disclaims any affiliation, association, connection with, sponsorship, or endorsements by such owners.

For permission to use material from this text or product, submit a request online at http://www.thomsonrights.com.

Library of Congress Cataloging in Publication Number is available. See page 188 for details.

For more information about our products, contact us at:

Thomson Learning
Academic Resource
Center 1-800-423-0563

Thomson Higher Education
5191 Natorp Boulevard
Mason, Ohio 45040
USA

ACKNOWLEDGEMENTS

The authors express appreciation to the many individuals they have worked with over the past several years. To Kent G. Stephens, Ph.D., who was one of the initial researchers to use the principles of Fault Tree Analysis in examining priorities in human and human/technical systems, we offer our indebtedness. In addition, we express gratitude to Craig Johnson for his creative and ingenious programming of the algorithm used in the PriorityPath® process. There were also many employees of Sage Analytics International Inc. who provided significant insights, testing, and suggestions for improvement of the processes now employed. We would like to thank Eric Green, Michael Czinkota, and Interlink Capital Strategies for guiding us through the final stages of publication. Furthermore, we also acknowledge the U.S. Army's Training and Doctrine Command for their validation of the algorithm and methodology now used by PriorityPath®. The authors also appreciate the efforts of Kathy Frandsen, Lynn Giles, and Tim Robinson, who provided editorial assistance. Finally, we give thanks to our families who gave the encouragement and, in some cases, the technical assistance we needed to persevere in developing the processes that have proved to be so useful to so many clients.

Interlink Capital Strategies

Acting as the authors' agent and business advisor in getting this manuscript published, Interlink Capital Strategies, and one of its Managing Directors, Alan Beard, has been invaluable. Interlink Capital Strategies (www.i-caps.com), established in 1994 as Interlink Management Corp., is a Washington, DC-based consulting firm specializing in emerging market finance and international business development. Their managers are experts in international project financing, trade financing, raising private equity, business development, and marketing. They have successfully arranged billions of dollars of financing and used government advocacy and strategic industry relations to structure transactions worldwide. As part of their business activities, Interlink Capital Strategies has contributed to and co-authored several business publications. Specifically, Mr. Beard has edited and contributed to the writing of more than 25 books, including most recently *Terrorism & Personal Security, Inside the World's Export Credit Agencies,* and *Inside the World's Development Finance Institutions,* published by Thomson Publishing.

"*Finding the Priority Path* is universally applicable to any organization seeking to successfully align their structures, systems and culture in order to rise above ordinary effectiveness and achieve greatness. This excellent book provides a comprehensive pathway necessary for valid corporate transformation. A tremendous contribution."

Stephen R. Covey, author, *The 7 Habits of Highly Effective People* and *The 8th Habit: From Effectiveness to Greatness*

Table of Contents

About the Authors	xii
List of Figures	xiv
Foreword	xv
Preface	xix

PART 1 THE BASIS OF PRIORITYPATH® — 1

Introduction: The Need for an Alternative Approach — 3
- Minuteman Missile — 4
- Challenger — 5
- Analysis of Human Systems — 6
- The Terrorist Threat — 6
- Overview of This Book — 7
- PriorityPath® Briefly Defined — 8
- Different from Consulting — 9
- Different from Survey Methodologies — 10
- Exhaustive and Complete — 10
- Removing Barriers to Success — 11

1 What We Have Learned — 12
- Resident Wisdom in Organizations — 12
- Resident at ALL Levels — 12
- Three Critical Questions — 13
- Profiles of Priorities of Executives — 14
- Barriers to Communication — 14
- Mid-Management Barriers — 15
- Impacts on Corporate Culture — 15
- Impacts on Organizational Structure — 16
- Impacts on Conflict — 17
- A Manager's Source of Knowledge — 17
- Focus — 18
- Internal vs. External Experts — 18
- Organizational Values — 19
- Knowledge Management — 20

Table of Contents

	Beliefs and Assumptions: No Substitute for Knowledge	20
	Recognizing Competencies	20
	Situational Planning	21
	Creativity and Involvement: The Competitive Edge	21
2	**What Else We Know About Organizations**	**22**
	The Plateau Plague	22
	Your Organization as a Social System	23
	The "Military Appreciation"	25
	The REAL vs. the IDEAL	26
	The Action-Planning Sequence	27
3	**What Is PriorityPath®?**	**29**
	Rooted in Risk Management Theory	29
	Validation of Methodology	30
	Important Considerations Before You Decide	31
	Unique Benefits of the PriorityPath® Process	33
	Getting Ready for a PriorityPath® Project	34
4	**How We're Different from Traditional Approaches**	**36**
	Risk Analysis	36
	More about Surveys	36
	Differences in Statistical Measures	37
	PriorityPath® Project Contrasted with a Survey	39
	PriorityPath® and Delphi Studies	40
5	**The PriorityPath® Process**	**41**
	Who Can Benefit?	41
	Overview of the PriorityPath® Process	42
	A PriorityPath® Project: The Steps You'll Take	42
	Separating the Critical Few from the Trivial Many	50
	Actions to Resolve High-Priority Issues	50
	Summary Statement	51
	PriorityPath® Deliverables	51
6	**The Theory That Makes It Work**	**53**
	Force Field Analysis	53
	Measurement of Resisting Forces	55
	The Counterintuitive Approach	56

7 Divergent and Convergent Thinking:
   The Mathematical Foundation   57
   The Reliability and Risk Equation: $P(S) + P(F) = 1$ 58
   Working the Averages: Playing Both Sides of the Equation 60
   Skillful Use of "and" Logic Approaches   60
   Multiply Successes by Using "or" Logic Approaches   61
   Characteristics of "and" Logic and "or" Logic:
     Convergence and Divergence   62
   Lessons from the Civil War: Full Speed Ahead   64
   Burnside Bridges   64

8 Who—and How—We've Helped   67
   G8 Summit: Security Planning—Canada   69
   Privatization of Electricity Market—New Zealand   71
   Energy Services   73
   Strategic Planning—A Canadian Province   74
   Electronics Manufacturing   75
   Test Instrument Manufacturing   77
   Sydney Water Board—Australia   79
   Hong Kong Tunnel   81

9 Conclusion   83
   Opening Organizational Eyes   83
   Contacting Priority Systems®   83

PART 2   ANOTHER OPTION   85

10 The Abacus Version of the PriorityPath® Process   87
   Get Started by Getting Buy-In   88
   Draft a Mission Statement   88
   Engage the Project Leader   88
   Form a Steering Committee   88
   Select Representatives to Participate   89
   Prepare a Cause/Effect Diagram   90
   Let Participants Examine the Diagram   91
   Assign Weights   91
   Develop Remedial Activities   92
   Sample Three-Day Abacus Project   93

11 Translating Findings to Action: Where to Go from Here   94

Major Themes   94
Remediation Teams—Focus on System Improvement   95
The "Linking Pin": The Relationship of Remediation
and Theme Teams   96
Successful Team Management   96
Commitment of Key Personnel   97
Commitment of the Remediation Team   98
Focus on System Improvement   98
A Unified Plan   98
Training   99
Recognition, Gratitude, and Celebration   100
Communication   100
Theme Teams   100
Preparing Recommendations   101
How to Format Your Recommendations   103

APPENDICES   105

Appendix A   Instructions for Rating   107
Background   107
Rating Criteria   107
Rating Guidelines   107
Relationship among Issues   107
Timing   108

Appendix B   What Clients Have to Say   109

Appendix C   Partial Client List   111
Federal Government   111
State and Provincial Governments   111
Local Government   112
Schools and School Systems   112
Health Care   113
Commercial Clients   113

Appendix D   Project Summaries: Resolving Controversial and Complex Issues, Achieving Measurable Results   115
A. Commercial Clients   116
    A Commercial Airline   116
    Water Management Projects   117

Revenue Enhancement 117
System Rehabilitation 118
System Expansion 118
A Chemical and Fertilizer Company 119
A Canadian Power Generation Company 120
Planning a Hazardous Waste Facility and
 Rubber Reclamation Plant 121
Hazardous Waste Plant Expansion 122
Information and Communication Services 123
A Telecommunications Company 124
A Major, Worldwide Consulting Practice 124
Calgary Olympic Games 125
Projects in Medical Services 126
 Expansion of a Medical Clinic 126
 Nursing Shortage 127
 Standard Procedures 127
 Amalgamation of Medical Practices 127
Tasmania to Australia Power Transmission 127
A Gas Gathering and Processing Installation
 in North Africa 128
A Capital Investment Project 129
B. Military and Space Projects 130
 Deep Battle Plans 130
 M1A1 Abrams Tank 131
 Army Space Initiative Study (ASIS) 132
 New Zealand Defense Forces 133
C. Petrochemical Industry 134
 Achieving Rated Capacity 134
 Sour Gas Management 135
 Equipment Startup 137
 Project Management Priorities 137
 Environmental Units 138
 Computer Control System 139
 Startup of Expansion Plant 140
 Rand Corporation Review 140
 Loss Management 141
 Other Petrochemical Installations 141
  Safety 142
  Dyke Stabilization 142

x   TABLE OF CONTENTS

Sour Gas Management	142
Safety and Loss Management	143
Turbine Repair and Operation	143
Caisson Recovery Problem	144
Property Services	145
Alberta Energy Resources Conservation Board (ERCB): Three Projects	146
1. Pincher Creek Project	146
2. Hewitt Oil Processing Plant	148
3. City of Calgary Emergency Response Plan Modification	149
A Major Resource Company: Offshore Drilling	149
D. Government and Regulatory Agency Projects	150
Traffic Management/Bay of Fundy	150
Airport Safety and Security	151
A Workers' Compensation Board	152
Coordination of OH&S Services	153
Government Departments	153
Recreation and Parks Department	153
A Sister Department	154
Wildlife Management	155
Department of Environment	156
Department of Justice Project	157
A Government Shared Services Project	157
Industrial Safety	159
A Mine	159
A Hospital	159
Safety in the Oil Fields	160
A Major Housing Authority	161
Tauranga District Council	163
Gisborne District Council (GDC)	164
Hastings City Council	165
City Planning for Wanganui	166
A Mid-Sized City Police Department	166
E. Education	167
Student Achievement	167
Modification of School Grant Structure	168
Amalgamation of School Boards	169

University IT Systems	171
University Student Services	171
F. Volunteer Agency Projects	173
An International Relief Program	173
A Volunteer Rescue Squad	174

Appendix E Executive Summary, Columbia Accident Investigation Board   175

Appendix F Example PriorityPath® Chart   179

References Related to Team Activity Consulted: Further Reading   181

Index   183

About the Authors

Bryant L. Stringham, Ph.D., Partner, Priority Systems®

Dr. Stringham received his B.Ed., M.Ed., and PH.D. in educational administration from the University of Alberta in Edmonton, Canada. Following several years of teaching and administrative experience, he became Director of Field Services for the Alberta Department of Education, where his staff advised school board personnel on financial management and maintenance of quality instruction in classrooms. During this time he evaluated British educational methods for Canadian use; rewrote the Alberta School Act; was a guest lecturer at the University of Alberta, University of Birmingham, and Sheffield Polytechnic in England; and published articles in the areas of educational legislation and organization. His doctoral dissertation in the field of public policy development has been used as a university reference text.

Since 1979, Dr. Stringham has directed PriorityPath® projects concerning policy development, organizational structure, risk management, increased productivity, project management, conflict resolution, needs assessment, and planning. He has provided HRD specialty services for numerous educational and industrial organizations. Clients such as the governments of Canada, Alberta, and the Northwest Territories—as well as numerous corporations including but not limited to Westinghouse, Chevron, Syncrude Canada, Esso, and Petro-Can—have benefited from his consulting services.

Dr. Stringham has been a featured speaker for numerous government, management, environment, waste management, and education conferences. He has also been a presenter in a semiannual Industrial Risk Management Course sponsored by the University of Alberta. Through the years, concurrent with his professional responsibilities, he has occupied senior executive positions within a large community organization. He is currently a partner in the firm of Priority Systems®, where he continues to offer the PriorityPath® process to clients.

Jon D. Stephens, Partner, Priority Systems®

Jon D. Stephens' experience in systems development and execution is extensive. His undergraduate degree is in mathematics, and he has completed considerable postgraduate work in the field of operations research. From July

1964 to January 1966, he worked for the Kenetics Corporation in Solana Beach, California. While there he served as head of the Reliability Department, responsible for all failure mode and effect analyses. His assignment included the gathering of data and use of advanced statistical techniques related to loss prevention and reliability.

From February 1966 to September 1967, Jon was a System Safety Engineer at the Boeing Company in Seattle, Washington. While there, he was responsible for the development of advanced mathematical formulas used in resolving complex systems analysis techniques, including the mathematical proofs for the solution to Fault Tree Analysis. He was responsible for gathering, interpreting, and using statistical data on large aerospace programs, such as the Minuteman Missile System. His responsibilities included development of an advanced analog computer to solve complex fault trees. Later on, he was responsible for performing statistical analysis on employee systems.

Jon has been a guest lecturer at many conferences worldwide. His publications include:

- "Consideration of the Life Support System," 4th Annual Safe Symposium, San Diego, CA
- "Systems Safety Using Monte Carlo Methods in Fault Tree Analysis," The Boeing Company, Seattle, WA
- "Lambda Tau or Constant Repair Method for Fault Tree Analysis," The Boeing Company, Seattle, WA (this is the definitive paper on Fault Tree Analysis, which is still used extensively in the nuclear and aerospace industries)

Since early 1970, Jon has been involved in the development and use of PriorityPath® and its predecessors, which are an outgrowth of his systems engineering background. As part of that work, he has managed numerous applications of the system worldwide.

LIST OF FIGURES

Figure 1	The Plateau Plague	22
Figure 2	Organizational Dynamics	23
Figure 3	REAL/IDEAL Congruence Model	26
Figure 4	Schematic of Action-Planning Sequence	27
Figure 5	Comparison of Surveys and PriorityPath® Methodology	37
Figure 6	Example of the Quantification/Rating Instrument	46
Figure 7	Prioritized Results of the Sample Project	49
Figure 8	Schematic of Force Field Analysis	55
Figure 9	Initiating Theme Team Activities	96
Figure 10	Critical Event Rating Criteria	108

Foreword

As we've interviewed thousands of people in organizations of all sizes and types, we've often heard comments like these:

"*Whose* priorities?"
"Those are not *my* priorities!"
"No one listens to me—my opinion doesn't matter to anyone."
"Nothing will change—it never does!"
"This must be the next flavor-of-the-month program."
"Great—the blind are still leading the blind!"

Why? Because when an organization doesn't have a reliable way to determine priorities, it usually relies on the judgment of the person who has the most authority, who is the delegated spokesperson, who has the most dominant voice, or who is the most persuasive. Unfortunately, people who have critical knowledge about the essential priorities aren't consulted, don't have a platform from which to make their points, or simply remain silent—after all, input that is radically different or that goes against the official party line could result in personal jeopardy.

What happens? Executives, even those who say they want broad input, frequently (though inadvertently) operate within a climate that severely limits the contribution of their close associates. As a result, decisions about priorities tend to be made by the same person or small group of people. They tend to follow decisions that were made in the past—without taking into account the wisdom of seldom listened to stakeholders who often withhold vital information upon which future success depends.

This book breaks that pattern. It lets your organization and the people connected to it open their eyes and ears to the wealth of resident intelligence that tends to be ignored. It opens avenues to rigorous diagnosis—identification, prioritization, and generation of innovative solutions—by the people who know the inner workings of your organization. It opens the door to creative resolution of the issues that, if not addressed, will limit progress, waste resources, cause stagnation, or hasten the demise of your organization. It expands the vistas of everyone associated with the enterprise. It makes each person aware of possibilities and promises that can be achieved as the entire organization focuses on limiting barriers and renewing its commitment to success. It opens eyes to the best way of accomplishing objectives that until now have seemed to be just out of reach.

How important is it to have eyes opened? Almost everyone has heard the following traditional story; the legend of the blind men and the elephant has appeared in a variety of cultures—most notably Chinese, African, and Indian—for thousands of years. As you review this poetic account, consider its implications for your organization:

The Parable of the Blind Men and the Elephant, John Godfrey Saxe

It was six men of Indostan
To learning much inclined,
Who went to see the Elephant
Though all of them were blind,
That each by observation
Might satisfy his mind.

The First approached the Elephant
And, happening to fall
Against his broad and sturdy side,
At once began to bawl:
"God bless me, but the Elephant
Is very like a wall!"

The Second, feeling the tusk,
Cried, "Ho! what have we here
So very round and smooth and sharp?
To me 'tis very clear
This wonder of an Elephant
Is very like a spear!"

The Third approached the animal
And, happening to take
The squirming trunk within his hands,
Thus boldly up he spake:
"I see," quoth he, "The Elephant
Is very like a snake!"

The Fourth reached out an eager hand,
And felt about the knee:
"What most the wondrous beast is like
Is very plain," quoth he;
"Tis clear enough the Elephant
Is very like a tree!"

The Fifth, who chanced to touch the ear,
Said, "Even the blindest man
Can tell what this resembles most;
Deny the fact who can:
This marvel of an elephant
Is very like a fan!"

The Sixth no sooner had begun
About the beast to grope
Than, seizing on the swinging tail

That fell within his scope,
"I see," quoth he, "the Elephant
Is very like a rope!"

And so these men of Indostan
Disputed loud and long,
Each in his own opinion
Exceeding stiff and strong.
Though each was partly in the right,
They all were in the wrong!

"JOHN GODFREY SAXE." *LoveToKnow 1911 Online Encyclopedia.* © 2003, 2004 LoveToKnow.

Now consider a different twist to the fable. What a difference it would make if each blind man could suddenly "see" how his experience fit as a part of the whole! Each person would then be able to "see" the entire elephant.

People who are in and associated with today's organizations often act like the blind men examining the elephant. It is critical that eyes are opened so that every person, including executives, can recognize the different perspectives, beliefs, and perceptions of all of his or her associates and use their collective wisdom to build the organization.

Within the pages of this book you'll learn of a scientifically validated method for opening eyes and expanding the vision of people connected with your organization. We know that it will work for you, because it has been used successfully in organizations of every type. It opens eyes to critical, largely overlooked sources of information that create synergy as viewpoints are shared and that generate sufficient energy to focus organizational activities on achieving success.

NOTES

This book contains many references to Priority Systems®, the registered name of the organization that currently performs the PriorityPath® process. The names of both the process and the company have changed over the years. In some instances, the work attributed to Priority Systems® was performed by a predecessor company but the process is essentially the same.

Many organizations are cited as users of the PriorityPath® process. These users have based their decision to use these processes on several criteria. Most of the users are organizations that operate in an exemplary manner. They have used PriorityPath® to further refine their already successful approaches by involving management, staff, customers, and other outside people in determining the directions that will further enhance their successes. Some of these organizations have used the process to focus upon areas that are in need of immediate attention so that unplanned, negative consequences need not be experienced. We view their use of these principles as an effort to remain successful and to fight any tendency toward complacency.

Preface

We pioneered the development of the analytical system described in this book. Our combined experience in systems development and execution is extensive and cumulatively spans more than 50 years. Throughout the experience, a number of other people have also been involved in developing and refining the process.

The struggle to develop PriorityPath® has been long and hard, with many uphill skirmishes. In a world devoted to pursuing success at any cost, the concept of looking at inhibitors, causes of problems, and potential failures seems foreign. But what could be more positive than avoiding hazards and pitfalls? We have used this system in a wide variety of applications—and we have consistently found that identifying and avoiding known and potential barriers is a significant factor in generating innovative approaches to organizational improvement. In fact, this system may well be the next major opportunity for achieving quantum improvements within progressive organizations in the most effective and efficient way.

Several U.S. government agencies, as well as private sector organizations, have reviewed available technologies and approaches that claim to yield outcomes similar to those we produce. Every review has concluded that our process is unmatched when it comes to identifying and resolving critical issues.

For example, the U.S. Army Training and Doctrine Command (TRADOC) evaluated numerous methodologies that would allow the Army to prioritize the deficiencies in their mission objectives and to determine potential failure points. In an extensive review, TRADOC evaluated our system along with methodologies offered by Vector Research, Operations Research, General Dynamics, Rumson Corporation, and Imperial Oil.

The result? The Army determined that our system not only was highly effective as a systems improvement tool, but that it couldn't be replicated. In fact, the Army found that most of the other methodologies used *descriptive statistics* to describe the nature of individual deficiencies and show the degree of consensus about their placement on a priority list. Our process was the only one that *mathematically* considered interactions among related issues and produced an integrated, prioritized list of deficiencies that show relationships among factors across critical areas based on *probabilistic statistics*. The

Army concluded that our process is so unique that it qualifies to be designated as "sole source."

As part of their review, Army mathematicians and computer specialists examined and tested the validity and reliability of the original mathematical formulae we used in our software, as well as the software itself. They confirmed the validity and reliability—as well as the unique nature—of the formulae and software. The Army also tested whether the process was robust enough to calculate the right answer even if it was given poor or deliberately misleading input data. Army testing determined that it was. As a result, our methodology has been acknowledged as a sole source process not only by the United States, but by governments in Canada and New Zealand as well.

A follow-up review by TRADOC in 2004 confirmed the judgments made in their earlier assessment of the process.

PART 1
THE BASIS OF PRIORITYPATH®

Endorsements

"In my experience, Priority Systems® . . . reliably compares profiles of priority among key individuals and major groups. . . . Results translate into action rapidly due to the deep involvement of all of the individuals and groups that are affected by the area under examination. My decision to use them (repeatedly) is based on my experience that their analytical system produces actionable results in ways that I have not experienced with any other analytical approach."

Gary Holden, *CEO and President, ENMAX Corporation*

"Arriving at mission-critical business goals involves aligning and managing resources. This is the essence of success! Recognizing, prioritizing, and eliminating the most critical business obstacles assures business predictability and certainty, creating stakeholder unity and alignment. Failure avoidance is the essence of sustainable growth and is the most positive means of enhancing success."

Skip L. Holland, *Senior Vice President, Managing Executive, Program Management, MWH Global, Inc.*

"PriorityPath® provides the elusive key to tapping into the business knowledge and inherent wisdom that resides within an organization. Despite its comprehensive nature, the process surprisingly requires minimal staff involvement and time. I have seen it produce extraordinary results in projects where accurate judgments about the priorities of key individuals and groups are critical to the success of the venture being examined."

Morrin Hardy, *Managing Director, Sage Analytics (NZ) Ltd.*

"The challenge of competing priorities and personal agendas are systematically addressed leading to successful accomplishment of critical mission outcomes. The process provides a roadmap to achieving mission critical outcomes which appear at first to be un-resolvable."

Bruno Petrenas, *City Engineer, Tauranga, New Zealand*

"PriorityPath® gave us the ability to diagnose and prioritize our organization's issues which enabled us to align our efforts and accelerate our successes."

Lynn K. Giles, *Director of Human Resources, The Church of Jesus Christ of Latter-day Saints*

"From classroom curricula to terrorist threats . . . from New Hampshire to New Zealand . . . from earth movers to pocket pals—PriorityPath® brings all stakeholders together in a common effort to analyze, plan, and anticipate 'what could go wrong' in the course of critically important projects. One outcome is that the plan is owned by everyone whose buy-in and support are essential for success."

Kevin W. Sullivan, *Partner, Sullivan/Luallin Inc.*

"PriorityPath® was used to conduct a performance audit and gap analysis in the preparation of a strategic plan and performance management framework for shared services delivery. Involving over 1,000 stakeholders, it provided an objective assessment of the barriers to implementation, clearly separating fact from perception and assuring that the appropriate strategies to achieve a difficult mission were in place and supported. It accomplished in weeks what would otherwise have taken months, clearing the way for getting on with the rest of the job. Results continue to guide our efforts a year later."

Per Andersen, *Executive Director Business Strategy, Alberta Corporate Service Center, Government of Alberta*

Introduction

The Need for an Alternative Approach

As a naval disaster seemed imminent, Civil War Admiral David G. Farragut promptly gave the orders embodied in the famous command, *"Damn the torpedoes, Full speed ahead!"*

For nearly 150 years, Farragut's words have been used as a rallying cry whenever people have faced a difficult task. Those words have also been a hallmark of business planning. Executives routinely confront obstacles simply by forging ahead.

This approach has produced remarkable success. Sometimes just moving on is the right thing to do—and will be successful. But when there are too many obstacles, or the obstacles are too large, simply moving on can cause the organization to collapse. Think what the effects would have been in the many organizations that have "gone under" if executives had known what would happen by just "going on," and if instead they had properly assessed the implications and taken corrective or remedial action.

Although the Farragut order may still be given in today's Navy, especially in pressure situations, the *preferred* scenario is for Naval decision makers to get the most relevant and timely intelligence they can, to match that intelligence to assigned tactical objectives, to measure it against strategic goals, to coordinate it with other command authorities, and then to act—if it's not too late. It's easy to see that a command like Farragut's would seldom be given if it had to be preceded by all this evaluation and coordination. It's also easy to see that organizations need to figure out ahead of time how they will anticipate, quantify, and counter threats *before* they grow out of control and do irreparable damage.

This kind of situation isn't limited to the Navy. Everyone can encounter "torpedoes" that are just as devastating as those faced by Admiral Farragut. There are organizational torpedoes, family torpedoes, personal torpedoes, and societal torpedoes. A common business torpedo is corporate acceptance of inaccurate or incomplete information that results in poor decisions. Family torpedoes could include a house fire or a mortgage foreclosure. Personal torpedoes may be a sudden onset of illness or a loss of employment. Some societal torpedoes are downturns in the economy and the impact of terrorist activities. Few of these "torpedoes" depend completely on technical and mechanical components.

When you face torpedoes, you need to quickly figure out how to avoid the impact—to make sure that you can prevent damage. If you've already been "hit," your job is more involved; you need to figure out not only what caused the hit, but how to recover and, importantly, how to prevent the same thing from happening again. How effective you are in making those assessments will determine how successful you will be in the future.

While all kinds of torpedoes are important and can do significant damage, the purpose of this book is to address the torpedoes that threaten organizations and their people. It identifies a paradigm shift you'll need to make to discover, document, analyze, and attenuate your organization's torpedoes before they strike and do irreparable damage.

Minuteman Missile

While working as a system safety engineer for Boeing during the midsixties, one of our partners was assigned to work on the Minuteman missile system, which at the time was the primary strategic missile defense system for the United States. It was critically important to make sure that an inadvertent launch or accidental motor ignition never happened. If either of these *had* happened, civilization would have been changed forever. If an inadvertent launch had taken place and the missile had landed in Moscow, Idaho, the loss would have been awful but survivable. If, on the other hand, the missile had landed in Moscow, Russia, the results most likely would have been catastrophic worldwide. The thought of Russia unleashing its nuclear arsenal in retaliation was unthinkable.

It's clear why the government spent a fortune to avoid such a scenario. Existing systems analysis methods were used, and new techniques were developed. All of the systems and subsystems associated with the missiles were analyzed in great detail. Probabilities related to potential failures for each of the systems' "black boxes" were calculated. Even the cable connectors were analyzed to make sure that critical wires were far enough apart to prevent catastrophic accidental shorting. This thorough analysis and remedial effort resulted in a safer hardware system.

But there was lingering concern about the way people interacted with these highly technical systems. The possible human factors included any human contact with the hardware during installation, operation, and maintenance. The challenge quickly became how to make the *human* element foolproof—or at least how to minimize exposure to risks from human activity. In attempting to do that, Boeing analysts generally inserted a probability for the human interface into the calculations—a probability

Introduction • The Need for an Alternative Approach   5

that represented the best engineering judgment of the person doing the analysis.

Too often, that judgment simply represented compliance with some predetermined government criteria for human involvement. Since there was no rigorous analytical procedure that could derive accurate probability numbers for human-related issues, Boeing's subjective numbers were seldom challenged or opened to rigorous scrutiny. The engineers tried to make sure that the numbers could be defended rationally and that they had "face validity," but the mixing of objective and subjective probabilities confounded the result as they were derived from different mathematical bases. The assumption that all probabilities are objective also flies in the face of known logic; people behave subjectively. On the other hand, if the assumption is made that all the probabilities are subjective, then all of the testing used to derive mean-time-between-failures (MTBF) and mean-time-to-repair (MTTR) probabilities are subjective. This, too, is nonsense! The mixing of subjective and objective probabilities is simply inappropriate.

When the engineering reports of the systems examined by Boeing were reviewed, it was not the hardware systems that raised concerns. The human interfaces became the focal points of the reports.

Challenger

A high-profile example of the impact of human factors was demonstrated in a project involving NASA following the *Challenger* Space Shuttle disaster. After the explosion that killed seven astronauts, NASA discovered that one of the o-rings that connected the segmented booster rocket sections of the fuel tank had failed. As a result, hot, volatile gases escaped and led to the explosion that plunged the remains of *Challenger* into the ocean. The company that built the rockets came under the scrutiny of NASA. There was an obvious question: "Why don't we build a monolithic rocket? No o-rings would be required—and we would prevent the sequence of events that caused *Challenger* to explode."

The booster rocket builder used our process to compare the reliability of segmented rocket systems with monolithic (solid) systems; the results of the analysis were sent to NASA. The findings were clearly evident. First, there was no reason to abandon the segmented design; the technical difficulties associated with a monolithic design were much more risky and greatly increased the probability of future problems. As a result, NASA kept the segmented design, but made appropriate improvements to the design of the o-ring.

6 FINDING THE PRIORITY PATH

The second finding involved the weather. The temperature on the day of the launch was approaching zero degrees centigrade; a temperature engineers knew could cause the o-rings to lose elasticity—making it impossible for the o-rings to form an effective seal between segments. In fact, at that temperature there was a high probability that the o-rings would fail. Our analysis revealed that while the *Challenger* disaster was technically caused by the failure of the o-ring, an underlying cause was the human decision to launch the shuttle in near-freezing conditions. The o-rings simply performed as they would always perform in similar situations. Our recommendation was that *both* the o-ring connection system and decisions about launch conditions must be monitored and managed much more closely in the future.

The *Challenger* example clearly demonstrates the need to add new dimensions to the analysis of existing and future systems that have both a technical and human component. Analyses must examine human/machine and human/human interface issues with rigorous analytical tools appropriate for the human dimension.

Analysis of Human Systems

There are other compelling and current examples of how the human factor impacts the organization. The report of the causes of the *Columbia* disaster (see Appendix E, "Executive Summary, Columbia Accident Investigation Board") focused attention on the need for more rigorous, frequent, and comprehensive analysis of human/human and human/technical interfaces.

The Columbia Accident Investigation Board used six different Fault Tree Analyses to examine all of the technical systems in the orbiter. However, the actual causes of the incident were more strongly related to the human aspects of the program—things such as safety programs, organizational structure, culture, and resourcing, which were all nontechnical components of the overall program. The Board didn't identify specific analytical tools to prioritize these human elements because they're simply not found in common approaches to identifying and resolving problems of this kind. That's why we developed the PriorityPath® process; it brings visibility to critical conditions and makes people sensitive to issues that are not commonly known, are misunderstood, or have been ignored.

The Terrorist Threat

In possibly no other scenario is the human factor more prevalent than in the terrorist threat. Protecting communities throughout the world from terrorism is a matter of both personal and national survival. When considering the

Introduction • The Need for an Alternative Approach 7

issue of increasing security as a result of terrorist attacks worldwide, it is necessary to have rigorous tools for handling subjective behavior. First of all, terrorists do not behave *objectively;* they behave *subjectively.* The task facing security agencies worldwide will require a variety of analytical tools and methodologies to successfully contain and eliminate the international threat. There will be a place for economic and hardware analysis, but just as important—and perhaps even *more* important—will be the ability to analyze human/machine and human/human interface issues. Our process has the capacity to predict and prevent what might seem like an inevitable disaster, and the ability to forewarn is a major key to controlling and preventing terrorist activities.

It's not an easy task to predict and prevent terrorism. Terrorists are subjective people bent on the destruction of others, often without regard to themselves. Their targets can be chosen at random with the sole purpose of killing as many people as possible. There appears to be little reason for their actions, other than an irrational determination to promote a cause they consider important or fulfilling a religious purpose. A further complication is that data collected about their activities is largely subjective, and the analytical tools used to analyze hardware systems simply can't analyze this type of subjective data without risk that the results will be both inadequate and inaccurate. Serious errors can also be made in analyzing subjective data unless a rigorous and appropriate methodology designed to analyze subjective data is used.

As is obvious, most organizational problems involve people—human judgments and humans interacting with machines. This is likely to become an even greater factor as more complex issues and risks arise in the future—especially in connection with worldwide security issues. We at Priority Systems® recognized early the need for rigorous tools to analyze the human factor, and we began a twenty-year search for a solution. That search culminated in the development of the PriorityPath® process, an exclusive offering of Priority Systems®. While the process is continually being refined, it combines a methodology and technology comparable in rigor to that used to analyze hardware systems—but the primary focus of the process is to resolve issues associated with people as well as the interface of people with equipment.

Overview of This Book

As you read, you'll become acquainted with a highly effective approach to identifying, documenting, quantifying, prioritizing, and neutralizing factors that can result in the failure to achieve organizational goals. This approach is the PriorityPath® process. It produces a comprehensive organizational diagnosis targeted toward accomplishment of the specific purposes of the organization. Using this process, organizations have saved millions of dollars, prevented catastrophes, increased productivity, and accomplished a wide variety of other sought-after results.

PriorityPath® focuses all available resources on accomplishing organizational purposes. Through the process, organizational structures, policies, processes, procedures, and all internal and external functions are focused and aligned with each other and with the vision, mission, goals, and objectives of the organization. In an aligned organization, no individual or function operates at cross purposes with the goal of accomplishing the organization's set direction.

The PriorityPath® process works. You'll read about positive results in organizations that have used our pioneering technology. We consider projects to be successful when they help organizations achieve the purposes specified for the project. In one case, success may be marked by the reduction of serious injury to workers; in others, it may be to resolve organizational structure, security, productivity, or financial concerns.

So, you might ask, has our system ever failed? Something positive has come from every project we have undertaken, but the degree of success has depended on how completely our clients have implemented the solutions to the issues the process has helped them to identify. When our clients have made the effort to implement recommended solutions, amazing things have happened. In some instances, we have been awarded extended contracts to monitor and assist clients with remedial activity; in other cases, clients have come up with internal improvement solutions and have implemented them without further help from us.

PriorityPath® Briefly Defined

PriorityPath® analysis has its roots in risk engineering. Simply stated, it uses sophisticated mathematical algorithms to calculate normalized ordinal probabilities—rank-ordered measurements of the priorities of individuals and groups participating in a project. It discloses and diagnoses the most critical issues and risks facing the organization from the perspectives of the most knowledgeable people invited to participate in the analysis. It focuses and aligns people and resources upon resolving these priority factors so timely action can be taken to prevent degradation of organizational purposes, efforts, and effectiveness.

Different from Consulting

Although the process has many similarities with consulting, there are major differences between the two. Consulting is based on the premise that organizations need expertise from outside to analyze situations and perform critical services. While that is certainly true at least some of the time, many organizations can make better progress, at a more reasonable cost and with longer lasting results, by addressing critical issues internally.

Many organizations believe that consultants provide necessary services in specialized areas where the organization doesn't have resident expertise. This approach is appropriate when consultants transfer expert knowledge to the client during the period the consultants are engaged with the client. However, some consultants hope to create clients who are dependent over the long term, which is not necessarily beneficial for the organization.

In contrast, Priority Systems® adopts a balanced view. The beginning of a PriorityPath® analysis—the time during which information is gathered—could be considered consulting, but the process then rapidly shifts to providing help and access to diagnostic tools that the client can use independently. This analysis is similar to the *diagnostic process* used in medicine; doctors diagnose an illness before they recommend a treatment. Using a treatment without proper diagnosis can be disastrous to the patient. *Organizations also need diagnosis before treatment.* To move ahead without diagnosis can be expensive, wasteful, and may irreparably damage the organization.

The PriorityPath® process is designed to help organizations perform a comprehensive diagnosis from the perspectives of all stakeholders involved with the issues under examination. Remember the six blind men and the elephant? Our process avoids that outcome. It requires the focused participation and involvement of all concerned people as the critical issues and their causes are identified and prioritized. This is accomplished with little intrusion into the daily activities of participants through focused interviews and other efficient data-gathering techniques. Because the resulting information and priorities are derived from the contributions of stakeholders, the findings are accepted—instead of being arbitrarily dismissed, as are many reports prepared by external consultants. Involvement is a key element in building ownership of the outcomes of analytical processes. As clients use their own people to identify, prioritize, and address priorities and then to develop action plans, lasting commitment toward resolving issues increases—in most cases, dramatically. You'll be able to see how this has worked for many organizations as you read this book.

Different from Survey Methodologies

Just as PriorityPath® analysis is not consulting, it must also not be confused with survey work, which all too often is superficial and biased. Survey research has never been known for its rigor. Survey makers strive to be as objective as possible, but in reality most surveys contain many subjective elements. This is particularly true when surveys explore how respondents "feel" about certain issues. The biases of the survey makers are also reflected in the survey document. That bias can enter in the type of questions asked, the multiple choice options included, and the selection of what is relevant. Bias may also enter into the interpretation of survey results when survey administrators choose particular statistical approaches that fit predetermined outcomes.

Because of the danger of bias, survey results are often rejected and rarely produce remedial actions. Respondents frequently comment that the survey asked the wrong questions. Additionally, matters that are of interest to respondents are often not among those asked in the survey. Also, the interpretation of survey results may have been interpreted by the researchers to mean something entirely different from the reality that respondents face each day.

Exhaustive and Complete

In contrast, PriorityPath® analysis is exhaustive and complete. The rating instrument from which priorities are calculated contains *all* of the relevant data contributed by stakeholders who represent *every* area of interest. It does not contain judgments made by the outside analysts. The probabilities it calculates are derived from responses to all of the data contributed by participants. This avoids the interpretative bias common in surveys and eliminates the need for analysts to summarize input data into a few survey questions that tend to bias the results from the outset.

Where performance is measured, performance improves. The database prepared from information used in PriorityPath® projects can be used to reassess priorities at a later date—in essence, you can measure the progress being made in your organization by using the same database later. This shows where changes have occurred and is a good measure of the degree of improvement that has been made.

You might also want to reedit the database, recording changes that have occurred in your organization since the first analysis was completed. You can use this edited data to report priorities a second time. Because the labor-intensive part of the process will be less involved for the repeat analysis, the costs are significantly lower, making this an excellent, cost-effective way to measure progress over time.

Removing Barriers to Success

PriorityPath® analysis is used in business, government, military, religious, and educational institutions to ensure successful pursuit of organizational purposes as it identifies, diagnoses, and removes barriers to success. It pinpoints the priorities of knowledgeable individuals and groups within the organization about the severity of existing and potential problems and the effects that will occur by removing or neutralizing those problems. PriorityPath® provides a stable platform upon which plans can be developed and actions taken. Further, it can provide not only a snapshot of conditions within an organization at any particular time, but it can also be used on a continuing basis to monitor progress toward organizational goals.

An Abacus version of PriorityPath® analysis that does not involve the proprietary computer programs necessary to the full program is described in a later chapter. With this information, you can get immediate but limited benefits without outside facilitation. We have used this modified approach with a number of organizations and helped them achieve significant benefits.

Chapter 1

What We Have Learned

After conducting several hundred projects, one thing has become increasingly clear: the people in any given organization are the ones who can tell what is wrong—and which things are most important.

Resident Wisdom in Organizations

Put a little more elegantly, we have seen time and again that there is considerable resident wisdom about factors crucial to any organization within the collective memory, judgments, and experience of the stakeholders who are closely associated with the organization and its processes. That has been true in every organization with which we have worked. It is true in military organizations, where the culture is not particularly open to input from persons of lesser rank. It is true in government departments and agencies, where formal, hierarchical structures tend to limit open communications. And it is true in medical clinics, where professional staff are often closed to input from people with lesser professional qualifications.

Resident at ALL Levels

We've learned other things, too. Sometimes the people with the most information about an organization are the ones least listened to. In other words, those in positions where they are exposed to multiple currents of conversation and communications often have information that the organization as a whole doesn't recognize, but that is essential to its progress. Here's a great example: the personal secretary to a senior official is at the crossroads of the information flow. He or she is able to integrate information from multiple sources and very clearly see what should be done to resolve specific problems. People in executive positions, however, may act on incomplete information—without access to critical information that the executive assistant has. Although executives trust that associates will keep them informed about every issue that they perceive is critical, many people are not sufficiently secure in their association with executives and may not share this vital information.

Essential information about organizations that is known by people of lesser status in the organization is seldom understood by senior personnel, much less acted on. In most of today's organizations, the unspoken belief is that the boss knows all that needs to be known to keep the ship on course; it is the executive's responsibility to search out the information he or she doesn't know. Highly qualified senior executives have learned to do this. But our experience shows that, on their own, even the most enlightened senior executives can't clearly track more than 20 to 40 percent of the critical data their associates in the organization have.

Three Critical Questions

At PriorityPath® we have learned that we can find that "hidden information" by asking three general questions to a sampling of people from each level in an organizations:

- What should we be doing that we are not doing now?
- What problems now exist that must be resolved in order to accomplish the mission?
- What potential problems may be encountered as action is taken to try to accomplish the mission?

We have learned, too, that what happens next is critically important. In most organizations, people have figured out that input from the "troops" is seldom elicited or valued. People we have interviewed often want to be assured that their input will not be used to destroy their careers; they have seen firsthand that providing input that doesn't support the current management direction is not wise. As a result, most people stay silent.

They have valuable information, and they want to share it, but only in a "safe" situation—with a spouse, with neighbors over the back fence, in the coffee room with peers. They're often unwilling to share in an "unsafe" place—anywhere the information could actually have an impact. That's why the PriorityPath® process maintains a strict policy of nonattribution as we gather information; we provide a safe outlet for critical information, and we give organizations access to the insights of all included stakeholders without revealing sources so action can be taken to avoid problems before they occur.

We've learned that while the answers to our three questions are most revealing, we have to be careful; if the information is mishandled, chaos quickly results. For example, if people define major organizational deficiencies, and that information is used to identify and punish the contributors, the situation may be worse than if executives had not sought the opinion of their employees. The same thing happens if people offer opinions and then nothing is done as a result.

A major contribution of PriorityPath® is to manage the information we get from people in the organization. Critical information is gathered anonymously, without identifying the contributors, unless an individual gives permission or chooses to tell others what he or she has contributed. Analysis of the information reveals the priorities of *groups* of participants. It focuses the organization on addressing the most critical areas that people closest to the issues judge to be of high priority.

Profiles of Priorities of Executives

In some recent projects, and with full agreement of participants, we have prepared profiles of the priorities of individual members of executive teams. When such results are compared and contrasted with the priorities of the various divisions within the organization and with the collective priorities of the executive team, areas where there is agreement and differences about priorities become immediately apparent. Executive attention toward resolving these revealed differences makes it possible to secure the alignment and focus of executives with a precision that is not usually possible.

Barriers to Communication

When Priority Systems® first began to use the PriorityPath® process, we saw that barriers to communication existed in most of the organizations with which we worked. We figured that we would eventually identify the universal problems creating those barriers, and that we would be empowered to find universal solutions to those problems. But this has not happened. We learned instead that communication problems in each organization are largely different from those found in every other organization. The particular mix of people, experience, purpose, and situation makes each organization unique—just as human nature makes each individual unique. As a result, two highly similar organizations can face similar obstacles and impediments to success, but they will have completely different priorities. We know that while communication is a major issue in most organizations, the details—and especially the solutions—are always different from one to another.

Mid-Management Barriers

We have learned that almost all organizations suffer from what we call "mid-management barriers": people at all levels of the organization believe that one of their most important responsibilities is to filter the flow of information. They believe that information flowing up *or* down needs to be filtered before it can be passed on to the people either above or below them in the hierarchy. One contributing factor is that people who receive a promotion (or who are placed higher in the hierarchy) often believe the promotion occurred because they have superior intelligence to others in the organization. And so they edit information to make sure (in their minds) that the correct message is being sent. They believe that they are fulfilling expectations. This can become a major problem.

We have learned that these mid-management barriers often become institutionalized to the detriment of the entire organization. It's easy to see how: a critical communication is filtered out before it gets to decision makers or to employees down the chain of command who have a need to know. There are some possible solutions to this barrier, and we've seen creative ways of dealing with it. We've learned that just as in barriers to communication, there is no universal solution to mid-management barriers. What works in one situation will not necessarily work in any other.

Impacts on Corporate Culture

We have learned that the culture of most organizations can be improved through open and honest communication of issues. Employees often think it's too risky to openly state opinions *unless* those opinions are welcomed and they have previously seen efforts being made to address legitimate concerns. We remember one creative solution adopted by a large organization to more fully leverage a practice that had long been part of its standard operation. For years, each manager had held a "Daily Dependability Meeting" with his or her immediate subordinates and selected people from throughout the organization to attend. The rotation resulted in each employee attending a meeting approximately every six weeks. The responsibility of the employees who attended was to return to colleagues and communicate what was discussed in the meeting.

When we came on the scene, we thought the meetings were a great idea—but our work changed the agenda of the meetings. Instead of being a standard meeting where management delivered instructions, managers began the meetings with a review of what had gone wrong the previous day.

This was followed by a brainstorming session to generate ideas of how to prevent the same thing from happening again. Next, the schedule for the day was reviewed, with particular attention given to meeting any unusual conditions they knew they must face. (For example, conditions that could arise from forecasted inclement weather were addressed to make sure that measures were taken and assignments given to deal with resulting pressures.) Finally, the daily review of routines focused on eliminating problems and barriers. The new meeting agenda was patterned after the data-gathering phase of a PriorityPath® analysis (described in Chapter 5, "The PriorityPath® Process").

After several months of following this new agenda, the senior manager noticed that changes had occurred in the organization. Instead of sitting in a meeting giving orders, he was able to spend an hour in a session designed to prevent problems—and then spend the rest of the day walking around, visiting all parts of the operation and making sure that attention to problem prevention was a priority. The financial savings to the organization were significant.

We have learned that part of the cultural heritage of many organizations is overconfidence by leaders that their directions will automatically be believed, followed, and acted upon. External indictors may even suggest to the leaders that this is the case. In reality, though, many competent people—including all those who think for themselves—know that unilateral pronouncements, especially those preceded by unilateral thinking, are generally not as beneficial as they could have been with the input of additional creative thinkers. By identifying and placing the previously hidden impediments where all stakeholders can see them, the PriorityPath® process invites exploration of innovative solutions. All other avenues are open. This kind of process lets managers gather and use the best creative thinking that exists within the organization.

Impacts on Organizational Structure

We have learned that organizational structure depends on the mix of individuals, the nature of tasks, the location, the traditions of the organization, and the typical response to the new and novel as well as a variety of personal decisions. We have learned that theoretical organizational structures are only a starting point; the details of structure evolve over time. The emphasis that an organization places on following a specific structure will be modified by the issues it will face; the tasks it will undertake; the people it employs; the history of its own and similar institutions; and the experience, needs, and demands that will be placed upon it. We have learned, too, that many forms of organizational structure can be effective when they are adapted to fit particular situations.

Impacts on Conflict

We have learned that a frequent response to conflict in an organization is to ignore the discord. That attitude—learn to live with it!—can be debilitating.

We have learned that we can expose underlying conditions, frustrations, needs, and wants in a nonthreatening way by using rigorous analytical procedures to identify resisting forces. We have learned that organizational conflict is often significantly reduced when we work with an organization—an unanticipated outcome of our involvement. Our process also has been extremely useful in changing the tone of labor negotiations to one of bargaining on the issues instead of fostering conflict between labor and management. One participant in a project told us that of all the conflict resolution systems he had seen as a manager and negotiator, none could match the success of the PriorityPath® process.

We have learned that whenever something goes wrong in an organization, someone is almost certain to proclaim, "If you had asked me, I could have told you!" The annoying thing is that they are probably right. This prompts the questions, Why don't people tell managers what they need to know? Why do employees always seem to tell managers only what they think the manager wants to hear?

A Manager's Source of Knowledge

We have learned that most often the answer is that many managers think they are uniquely endowed with the wisdom necessary to manage the business—something that can be characterized as the "Wizard of Oz" syndrome. While it may be true that a manager is brilliant, it is *also* true that others also have critical information that a wise manager urgently needs to know. Managers do *not* know everything, and they can learn much from other stakeholders. A person's position in the organization's hierarchy does not confirm unique knowledge or ability, guarantee competence, nor necessarily engender the trust of fellow workers.

Having said this, the climate in many organizations seldom encourages people to speak out. PriorityPath® helps the organization overcome this problem. When management authorizes a project, people soon learn that each person is expected to contribute the most critical information he or she possesses in a way that cannot be used to punish the contributor. Then as priorities are determined, these same people are given opportunities to contribute toward remediation of critical issues. The entire process engenders a spirit of cooperation and commitment to the goals the organization is working to accomplish.

We have learned that organizations benefit from accessing and using the knowledge of their stakeholders. Suppliers, clients, associated financial and accounting institutional representatives, interest groups, the media, regulatory agencies, and all other stakeholders associated with an organization often have significant information that is essential for executives to know. If there are mismatches in perceptions between the organization and its stakeholders, there is a need for greater involvement to expose gaps and misunderstandings. PriorityPath® captures this information, because we have learned that when such information is organized, formatted, rated, prioritized, and then acted upon, the status of the organization improves in the minds of all participants. Relationships with stakeholders improve. They become partners in working toward the greater success of the organization instead of being observers who are waiting for the chance to exercise their own self-interests. It is always wise to befriend potential detractors. The PriorityPath® process does that for organizations.

Focus

Most successful managers assume that everyone is moving in the same direction. After all, everyone is working toward accomplishing the same mission. Managers assume that everyone shares their vision and wants to achieve the same goals. Employees are informed by word of mouth or by directive that the direction is fixed, that it will result in success, and that their task is to move in accordance with the established policies and procedures.

We have learned that, unfortunately, there are often major differences in what management thinks its employees believe and what the employees themselves actually believe. Too often the bosses are marching to the south, while the troops are steadfastly pressing to the north. PriorityPath® maps these divergent journeys, showing precisely where the mismatches in orientation are. We then enable managers to redirect their own and their employees' efforts so they are all proceeding in a congruent direction. This ability to bring focus is one of our major contributions.

Internal vs. External Experts

We have learned that no one knows your problems like the people on the inside. Outside consultants simply can't know what is taking place inside the organizations they briefly visit. Some consultants try to overcome this problem by taking up residence in the organization—but this introduces another set of problems. The organization becomes dependent for direction on people who are "outside the family." The consultants may not share the objectives of the organization's leaders. The outside consultant may not share ideas about cost containment, may provide minimal direction, or may be able to serve only the small segment of the market that they know well. For reasons such as these, consultants are shunned by many organizations. We've often heard the sentiment, "If we can't do it ourselves, or hire permanent staff to teach us how to do it, we will be better off and even save money."

PriorityPath® often appeals to such organizations. Instead of coming to an organization to provide an outside assessment and deliver a prescription of what we believe needs to be done, we help people *inside* the organization focus on their emergent mission. Sometimes, at the direction of the client, we may ask a few well-chosen "outsiders" to participate. These would be persons who know intimate details of the organization. The process itself, however, is directed by "insiders" who focus the analysis on issues that people inside the organization determine need attention. Information is gathered from inside people and other selected stakeholders. It is rated for significance. When the priorities are reported, the remediation activity is coordinated and usually performed by "insiders." Inside operations are strengthened, and dependence on outside consulting is reduced. In situations where more expertise is needed before a problem can be solved, it is not uncommon to use outside organizations to help.

Organizational Values

We have learned that organizations develop internal mythologies about what is and is not legal, moral, or ethical. Collectively, these become the values of the organization. Sometimes, these evolving values lead organizations to tolerate practices that are questionable. A good example is how organizations interpret human rights legislation; some organizations that get caught breaking the law find that the culture of the organization blinded officials to the illegal acts they were committing, almost unknowingly. In every organization there is awareness of these kinds of situations as they develop. When an organization takes early action to identify, analyze, prioritize, and address such issues, as they do in a properly focused PriorityPath® program, these kinds of situations are rooted out at the source. Such organizations use the expertise and experience of their human capital.

Knowledge Management

We have learned that organizations generally have only primitive methods of preserving the knowledge and corporate memory that accumulates in every organization. The new field of knowledge management is addressing this issue, but ways of transferring knowledge are still unrefined. As a result, people who leave the organization often take critical knowledge with them—leaving the organization bereft of skills and information essential to the ongoing success of the organization. PriorityPath® projects that require people in critical positions to expose their deepest concerns, and then take remedial action to address those needs, ensure that the specialized knowledge upon which the success of the organization has become dependent will be perpetuated. In fact, we have helped numerous organizations aggressively address the area of knowledge management.

Beliefs and Assumptions: No Substitute for Knowledge

We have learned that popular, skeptical views of organizations and hierarchies are often more real than what organizational leaders believe is happening in their organizations. This happens despite the fact that structures and plans are usually based on solid principles of organization and organizational behavior. When leaders don't have a way to precisely measure what is happening within the depths of the organization, they act on what they *believe* is happening. They don't know how their associates view the same situations, but they often *assume* they know. Organizational leaders need a way to constantly monitor what is actually happening—it is very important to know what people are saying, feeling, doing, grousing about, suggesting, not doing, and how they are actually spending their time. PriorityPath® provides this capability to managers.

Recognizing Competencies

We have learned that many organizations don't recognize the capability of their employees. Because of this, little independent action by individual employees is either expected or tolerated. This is a major factor that causes staff turnover in even some of the most prestigious but highly controlled organizations. Use of PriorityPath® overcomes this problem.

We have learned that senior executives often get their information from a very limited group of people—and that the knowledge possessed by this small group does not reflect the depth of wisdom possessed by people throughout the entire organization. Bouncing ideas around is certainly mind expanding, but if it doesn't include the collective wisdom that resides in employee groups, any decisions that result will be less robust than they could be.

Organizations that limit their use of employees' knowledge are significantly wasting the human capital in which they have invested so much time, energy, and money to secure. CEOs should make sure that they do not limit their access to additional knowledge by letting small groups influence most of their decisions. The risk in doing so is that the decisions are probably tainted by personal bias or by people who have a narrow perspective. Also, executives who are not part of the discussion group may think their peers are receiving preferential treatment, or they may come to see those in the "inner group" as the competition instead of part of the team. Executives need a system in place that ensures they receive input from every legitimate source at their disposal. PriorityPath® is that system.

Situational Planning

Planning in organizations needs to be situationally based. It must reflect actual knowledge of conditions in the organization—not hunches, guesses, hollow proclamations, and imported mission statements that no one in the organization accepts. Because of what we have learned, PriorityPath® helps an organization focus on the areas of greatest need as perceived by individuals and groups that are closely associated with the enterprise. There is a corollary benefit; the people who are responsible for remediation are focused on resolving those areas of concern. In numerous projects, we have helped organizations identify loyal, competent employees who, through misperceptions, have been working against the best interests of the organization. Correcting their misdirected activity alone has been a significant benefit.

Creativity and Involvement: The Competitive Edge

The Priority Systems® process fosters creativity and requires a level of involvement that is not only extraordinary, but that is different from most analytical processes. The process is simple to understand and can be completed in a short period of time. It uses the expertise that you assemble, usually from within your own organization (and perhaps additionally from outside stakeholders who have expert knowledge and who you respect). These and the many other unique characteristics you'll read about make PriorityPath® a competitive-edge instrument for your organization.

CHAPTER 2

WHAT ELSE WE KNOW ABOUT ORGANIZATIONS

Organizations exist to fulfill specific goals, objectives, missions, and visions. Those goals, objectives, missions, and visions can be considered a description of where the organization wants to be. People within the organization then take actions to move the organization from where it is to where it would like to be.

Sound good?

The Plateau Plague

Unfortunately, the hoped-for smooth path to the planned success seldom occurs. The organization then has to change the routines and procedures to accommodate unexpected challenges. Instead of experiencing the continual growth the organization expected, progress stalls. The "Plateau Plague" appears (see Fig. 1). The problem then becomes one of how to break the cycles that have interrupted the anticipated journey to success.

If you recognize your own organization in this illustration, you're not alone. But you're also not sunk. By identifying, documenting, prioritizing, and remediating the factors that are causing the deviation, the PriorityPath® process helps align the reality more closely with the plan than could be done in any other way.

Plateaus are scary—in addition to what they can do to your organization itself, your stockholders, executives, and employees start getting concerned when the organization hits a plateau. They know that unless value is continually added to the enterprise, the future can be bleak. It's possible to get off

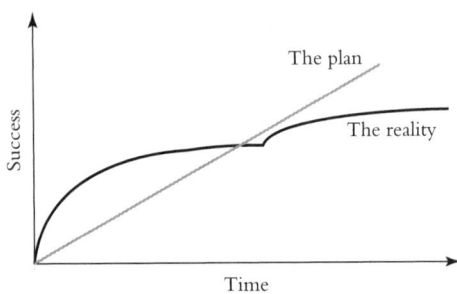

Figure 1 The Plateau Plague

the plateau, but it takes the right approach. PriorityPath® analysis lets you conduct an internal inspection; ascertain with precision where the roadblocks are, and focus renewed activity on the priority actions you need to take to move onward and upward. By taking the recommended periodic snapshots of conditions, you are empowered to continually redirect efforts toward overcoming barriers that evolve. As a result, you can create a smooth upward path that includes continual improvement, organizational alignment, and maximum prosperity.

Your Organization as a Social System

The following chart (see Fig. 2; initial concept developed by Getzels and Guba[1]) shows the common major interests of organizations and the priority interests of individuals who work in organizations. Look familiar? You can see that the interests of your organization are significantly different from those of the individuals who work in your organization. Both dimensions are important. Both have profound effects on the accomplishments of both your employees and your organization, making it imperative that a balance between the two dimensions always occurs. When either dimension receives undue emphasis, dysfunctions occur—and smooth operations are interrupted.

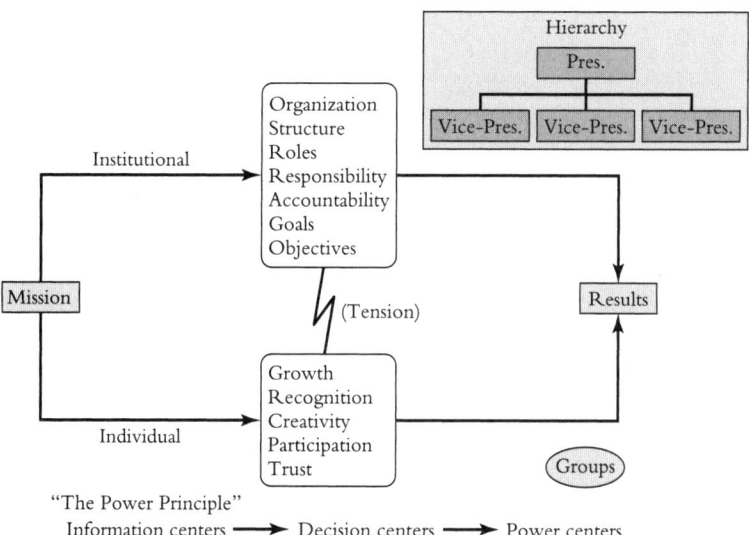

Figure 2   Organizational Dynamics

---

[1] Getzels, J., and Guba, E. *Social Behavior and the Administrative Process, School Review 65,* Winter 1957, pp. 423–441.

Here's how it works: Organizations usually emphasize things like roles, objectives, and goals, and they often use the hierarchical management structure. There are many desirable outcomes; this type of structure is particularly beneficial for specifying responsibility and accountability, for example. But a hierarchical system is not particularly effective in meeting the goals of individuals. People who want to progress and be creative find that working within some sort of informal group—such as a task force, committee, team, matrix structure, or inverted triangle structure—is more conducive to personal growth than is a hierarchy. If you focus on accomplishing only the institutional goals, you may create *tension* among people who, in addition to their commitment to the institutional goals, also have legitimate self-interests they would like to achieve in the workplace.

What's the answer? It is possible to strike a workable balance between accomplishing organizational requirements and providing an atmosphere in which personal growth can occur, but it requires that management and the members of both formal and informal groups are properly empowered. If a group is given tasks that are insignificant either to the group itself or to management, the group simply will not function well. If a group becomes too strong, on the other hand—with lengthy assignments that give its members exclusive access to critical information—the power the group acquires may disrupt normal corporate functions and may become threatening to managers.

When an informal group gains sufficient strength such that it threatens your management, you have an example of what is popularly referred to as The Power Principle. Here's how it works: A group that collects critical information independent from your organization's hierarchy frequently assumes or is given responsibility to make decisions, or at least to influence decisions, because of the unique knowledge it has. The group becomes a Decision Center. Once that happens, it's just a short step to becoming a Power Center, an informal source of power, placing unwanted pressure on the hierarchy and creating conflict within your organization. What usually happens in a case like this? Management suspends group activity. That generally restores management control—but it generally frustrates the group members. We've seen the resulting disruptions this condition causes destroy morale in many organizations.

What can be done, then, when you see a group becoming a Decision Center? We've helped a number of organizations strike an optimum balance between access to knowledge and distribution of power. How? By precisely measuring the priority needs of both the individuals and the organization as a whole. Management is then able to focus on cooperative means to resolve the priority issues that are of greatest consequence to the entire organization. This gives meaning to the statement you've undoubtedly heard before, "You gain control by letting go!"

The "Military Appreciation"[2]

In looking at your organization, you might gain insight from the military. The British Military Academy (Sandhurst) teaches an approach to problem solving, which has been adapted for use in other situations, called the military appreciation. One of Sandhurst's most famous graduates, Sir Winston Churchill, was a proponent of this system.

In planning a campaign, whether the purpose is offensive or defensive, the academy teaches that a military appreciation provides the guidelines for ensuring success. Here it is, in simple terms:

1. Select an objective and write it as clearly as possible.
2. List all the known factors that could keep you from attaining your goal.
3. Examine the considerations that may affect your attainment of the goal from "our" point of view.
4. Generate and accommodate the considerations that may affect your attainment of the goal from the point of view of the "enemy."
5. Examine all possible courses of action that are open.
6. Analyze all your options.
7. Formulate your plan.
8. Before you implement your plan or allocate any people or materials to it, mentally walk several hundred yards into enemy territory to reexamine the adequacy of your plan through the eyes of the enemy.
9. After you address any deficiencies in your plan, marshal people and materials in a way that makes it possible to implement your plan.
10. Implement your plan.

When you've completed all ten steps—and if there are no significant hazards, problems, or deficiencies that you have not identified and fixed—you can expect success.

---

[2] *The Military Appreciation.* Personal communication with a graduate of the Royal Military College, Sandhurst, England.

There are many parallels between the military appreciation and PriorityPath® analyses. Both use precise, orderly, and systematic methods to understand potential weaknesses, deficiencies, and problems while specific action plans are being prepared. The PriorityPath® process, however, facilitates even greater precision in planning by providing your managers with a proven technological decision-support system. Decision makers will be increasingly confident when they can see actual measurements of how significant each factor is to people and groups in your organization. Your managers don't have to rely solely on making subjective judgments about where consensus on issues exists. You—and your managers—know the priorities of each group, and those priorities can be accommodated in decisions that are made.

The REAL vs. the IDEAL

There's another way of looking at the challenges that occur when you are working toward achieving a perfectly operating organization (see Fig. 3). The IDEAL represents the conditions when every part of the organization is working according to plan. Every part of the ideal organization is positive and is purposely focused on meeting predetermined, positive outcomes. The REAL, on the other hand, represents the reality that organizations face. There are unresolved issues, problems, and barriers—most of them unanticipated. Fortunately, most organizations have a substantial overlap between the REAL and the IDEAL—an overlapping area that represents

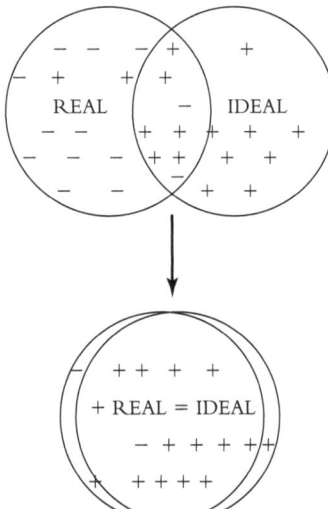

Figure 3 REAL/IDEAL Congruence Model

those parts of the organization that are operating well. Your goal, then, is to make that overlap as large as you can.

There are a number of things you can do to increase the size of the overlap between REAL and IDEAL, such as decision making, formulating policy, planning your strategy, and problem solving. (When you learn the mathematical foundations of PriorityPath®, you'll see that these processes emphasize increases in driving forces, or maximize the success enhancement side of the $P(S) + P(F) = 1$ equation.) The large measure of success that exists in our corporate and public institutions is due to the considerable expertise within organizations in applying these models.

While you want to make sure there is significant overlap between the REAL and the IDEAL, don't go too far. If you try to force the REAL and IDEAL together without removing the negative factors, you'll be met with substantial resistance. Why? The negative forces and pressures in the REAL world resist the positive new factors. However, when your organization takes specific steps to remove the negative pressures and factors, you'll create enough space to accommodate all of the positive factors you want to add. This scenario is shown by the nearly congruent set of circles at the bottom of Figure 3.

PriorityPath® helps you identify and remove the negative factors—creating the space you need for the positive factors that will move your organization closer to optimum conditions.

The Action-Planning Sequence

When your organization gets involved in planning, it will probably go through some well-defined and predictable steps (see Fig. 4) that are typical of most organizations.

First, you will determine the mission that will guide your plan. Next, you will create a plan that will specify the actions that will be needed to get the expected results. Your organization will then implement the plan.

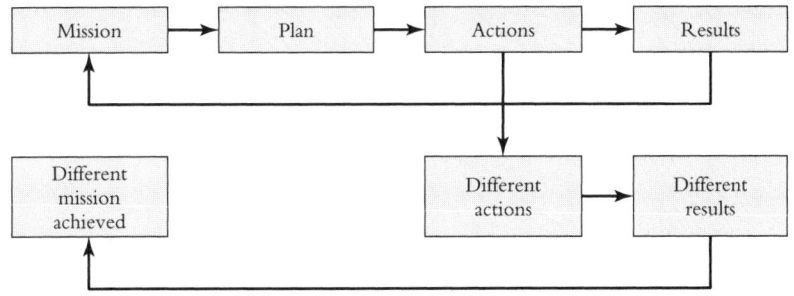

Figure 4 Schematic of Action-Planning Sequence

The process seems simple, but things don't always go as planned or expected. When you compare your results with the initial mission—what you were trying to accomplish—you may find that your results are different from what was anticipated. In other words, something different was achieved. Your organization migrated toward other goals, primarily because it took different actions than were specified in the plan. As a result, your organization actually achieved a different mission.

What happened actually has little to do with your mission or plan—they may both be perfectly satisfactory. The problem arises when your organization takes actions that don't follow the plan or the mission. When you try to address and fix these sorts of problems, then, you need to concentrate not on the mission or the plan, but on the actions being taken in your organization.

A classic example of this phenomenon can be seen in *The Bridge on the River Kwai* by Pierre Boulle,[3] a novel recounting the experience of the indomitable British officer Colonel Nicholson who was captured by the Japanese during World War II. The railway bridge that Nicholson and his men were forced to build across the River Kwai became Nicholson's means of preserving his organization and inspiring his men with the will to survive. A triumph of planning and strategic vision, the bridge became a symbol of Nicholson's humane and rational leadership even as it became a target of the British commando team sent to destroy it. The universal goal of prisoners of war to escape if possible was submerged by the Colonel's determination to finish the bridge.

PriorityPath® projects will give you real-time help to avoid this situation in your organization. We identify shifts in goals and actions as they are occurring, permitting you and your management team to decide what you need to do to keep your organization focused on your original or evolving mission.

---

[3] Boulle, Pierre. *Bridge Over the River Kwai,* New York, Bantam Books, 1979.

Chapter 3

What Is PriorityPath®?

PriorityPath® is an innovative, unique, and proprietary strategic alignment methodology based on proven risk engineering principles and mathematics. The process has been proven to work with machines, but its real value is in analyzing risks and issues that involve people. In basic terms, it is used in an organization to:

- identify the critical risks and problems, including those encountered in developing strategic plans, producing products, or delivering services;
- evaluate the probable impact of those risks;
- prioritize the risks—rank them in order of significance; and
- figure out a way to attenuate or remove the risks to facilitate productive change.

With its ability to anticipate and measure the effects of human reasoning, PriorityPath® gives managers at all levels a substantial tool they can use to quantify issues involving human judgment. As a result, managers have a tool that lets them identify, quantify, and resolve complex human issues in the organization. It provides a rigorous system of analysis that handles man/machine issues, and is equally powerful in analyzing human activities that don't involve machines—such as planning, measuring student academic achievement, making organizational assessments, dealing with human resource matters, and a host of other social and economic issues. Because these tools are powerful in analyzing any meaningful human endeavor, those who use them are responsible for their ethical use.

Rooted in Risk Management Theory

PriorityPath® analysis has its roots in risk management, but it goes far beyond the typical limits of traditional risk management. It lets you quantify the impact of issues of all types—including risks—in a way that shows what you can expect if things don't change. It works as well on single issues as it does on large clusters of issues.

PriorityPath® is a refinement and extension of recognized reliability engineering approaches, but it takes into account the extreme variance that happens when you consider subjective data—in other words, when people are involved. It calculates the likelihood that you might need to take corrective action. It accurately quantifies the judgments of involved people, ranking the priority of issues from the perspectives of those who know the issues best. It gives an objective analysis of operational and management concerns, as well as technical matters. It is a tool that sets a framework for taking effective and economical action to resolve the most critical issues that face your organization.

The specific algorithms that describe the mathematical model we use are proprietary and are beyond the scope of this book. They give us a unique ability; we are able to correctly rank the issues and risks in your organization. However, we also are able to predict the likely impact of those risks without introducing the inaccuracies that happen when statistical processes are improperly used to measure subjective data—in other words, people.

Our process avoids the problem of bias that can happen when calculating these complex probabilities. Proof of this came by using Mathematica®,[1] a comprehensive computer program from Wolfram Research, Inc. Mathematica performs thorough calculations by seamlessly integrating a numeric and symbolic computational engine, graphics system, programming language, documentation system, and advanced connectivity. We used it to test the match of input and output data in the PriorityPath® algorithms. Reliability was demonstrated by preparing scattergrams of all input data and comparing them with intermediate and final calculations of probabilities. The scattergrams correspond on a one-to-one basis. We've also confirmed face validity and reliability of results through experience with hundreds of clients who confirm that the judgments made in rating the significance of issues are faithfully represented in the final reporting diagrams and documents.

Validation of Methodology

In the preface of this book, you read about what happened when the U.S. Army's Training and Doctrine Command examined our system. They're not alone. For example, Esso Resources evaluated the mathematical formulations we use in our analysis process. As a result of that evaluation, Esso Resources went on to conduct a project for its operations in the Beaufort Sea and later circulated a review of the procedure throughout the Exxon-Esso

---

[1] Wolfram, Stephen. *The Mathematica Book, Third Edition*. From *The Mathematica Book* and other Mathematica documentation. Web version generated from Mathematica notebook source by Wolfram Research electronic publishing technology.

network of companies. On the strength of Esso's evaluation, their partner Syncrude Consortium has completed eight projects using our analysis.

Consider a few other examples: The U.S. Bureau of Indian Affairs hired the Stanford Research Institute to do a technical evaluation of the PriorityPath® process. Following Stanford's review, the Bureau of Indian Affairs contracted for an entire series of projects.

The Medical Division of the U.S. Veterans Administration had the analysis process evaluated by three technical experts. A number of Veterans Administration hospitals then used the analysis process as part of their accreditation process.

Finally, the Nuclear Utilities Service Corporation in Pittsburgh had a thorough evaluation of our process done by the former head of Fault Tree Analysis projects at the U.S. Nuclear Regulatory Agency. Following the evaluation, the company decided to use our analysis system.

Important Considerations Before You Decide

Maybe you're ready to find out what the most compelling issues are in your organization—but how do you decide which system is best to use? The following concepts are critical, and need to be part of any analytical approach to identifying and ranking your organization's priorities.

Related Groups. Issues and risks *must be* identified in related groups. Why? We've found that a seemingly innocent risk combined with another seemingly innocent risk can result in a *major* risk. When the impacts of issues and risks are considered independently instead of in related groups, no one picks up on the potentially serious interactions. In contrast, the PriorityPath® approach considers issues and risks within their context and calculates the interactive relationships among related issues.

Multiple Criteria. It is critical that multiple criteria be used to decide how much emphasis should be given to any one issue or risk. Simply saying that a particular risk is critical can mean many different things to different people. When judging the actual and potential impact of any issue or risk, several criteria should be used—including judgments of importance, the degree of expertise of the person making the judgment, the frequency with which the issue or risk occurs, and the ease with which the issue or risk can be fixed or avoided. When fewer criteria are used, you can easily miss many factors that later prove to be pivotal. PriorityPath® is the only system we know of that uses all four of these criteria.

Proven Analytical Techniques. Before they use a particular system, many organizations insist that independent organizations validate the algorithms that will be used to quantify the impacts of issues and risks and to set priorities. If you don't use validated assessment systems, it's likely that you will expend time, energy, and money identifying and resolving the wrong issues. In the final analysis, without proven analytical techniques, you'll be getting the personal opinions and biases of the people who are administering the analysis—and those biases and opinions generally override the valid concerns of the many informed people who work in your organization. The PriorityPath® system has undergone rigorous validation, as discussed earlier.

Risk Management Requirements. Risk analysis systems and other methods of calculating priorities need to meet the requirements for risk management projects specified by the U.S. Department of Energy,[2] Office of Integrated Risk Management. Briefly, those principles are:
- Risks should be described both qualitatively and quantitatively.
- The rationale for expressing risk judgments should be articulated.
- Risk assessments should encompass all appropriate hazards to health, the environment, and the enterprise.
- Risk management programs should analyze risks, benefits, and costs (direct and indirect, quantifiable and nonquantifiable) and should include prevention strategies.
- Risk programs should compare risks, grouping them into broad categories of concern (for example, high, moderate, and low).

Consistent Follow-Through. Priority-setting programs that involve people central to the operation of your organization shouldn't be started unless you know there will be consistent follow-through to a remediation stage. If your employees and close associates identify and prioritize the issues they believe need to be addressed, your credibility will be destroyed if nothing is then done about those issues. You've probably heard it before: "Don't ask for my opinion if you don't really want to do anything about it."

Trust. Trust and confidentiality are the hallmarks of a successful priority-setting activity. The information contributed by each

---

[2] U.S. Department of Energy. *Risk Principles: Risk Assessment, Management, and Communication and Priority Setting*, prepared by the Office of Integrated Risk Management, 2003.

participant must never be attributed to that person without their approval—otherwise, people in your organization will never open up and talk about the issues they see as having an impact on your organization.

A tough list? Yes, but it's an important one. PriorityPath® is the only priority-setting process we are aware of that meets all of these requirements.

Unique Benefits of the PriorityPath® Process

There are at least a dozen unique benefits for your organization when you use the PriorityPath® process:

1. It saves money and focuses stakeholders by breaking down the critical barriers to success.
2. Stakeholders are willing to participate in a nonattributional setting and appreciate the opportunity to contribute to the betterment of the organization.
3. It provides organizations with quality information quickly. It is not a time-consuming and drawn-out process.
4. It provides a comprehensive organizational diagnosis of the most critical issues very quickly.
5. It boosts employee morale and organizational health because stakeholders at all levels are allowed to contribute to the process of identifying, prioritizing, and solving the organization's problems.
6. The exercise of prioritizing your organization's issues and risks focuses your organization on the most critical areas of need so resources can be most wisely used—saving money in the process.
7. Quality decisions are the natural result of quality information.
8. Faulty assumptions upon which decisions have been based are quickly exposed by the results of projects.
9. Gathering information about issues and risks anonymously allows stakeholders to contribute that information without fear of reprisal. This provides you and your managers access to quality information that would otherwise be unavailable.
10. Employees feel a rebirth of energy when they are asked for their judgments. They feel valued and believe the organization genuinely respects them and values their opinion.
11. It is the fastest way a new CEO or manager can get up to speed with the organization because it provides a systematic way of reconnoitering a new situation. In a period of just a few weeks, new

managers will know much more than usual about the conditions within the organization, as well as coming to know the expectations and beliefs of the personnel with whom they will be working.

12. The system produces many benefits through the process itself. It creates a new level of trust between your managers and their employees. It opens lines of communication. It identifies major weaknesses or errors that may have been hidden or ignored for years. Most of the time, it results in considerable cost savings, which lets clients become more profitable; in other cases, it saves time by identifying and eliminating nonproductive activities. It has also led to streamlined organizational structures, realigned processes and goals, and helped streamline the mission of the organization more effectively. The PriorityPath® system lets an organization see precisely what is happening on the inside from various points of view.

Getting Ready for a PriorityPath® Project

Preparation is essential in any endeavor—and the exercise of identifying and prioritizing issues and risks is no different. When you're considering a PriorityPath® project, take a look at what you'll need to do to get the organization ready:

Get a Champion. Before a PriorityPath® project starts, your organization's decision makers—such as CEOs and senior executives—need to know what the process involves and what benefits to expect. You'll need an internal champion, someone who is credible and trustworthy, who is formally recognized throughout the organization, and who is given sufficient authority to make sure that the process will be pursued with energy.

Get on the Same Page. All of the senior managers and other officers in your organization should be united and consistent in their message to employees about the importance of—and their personal support of—the PriorityPath® Project.

Educate People. Once decision makers understand the process, give the rest of your organization an overview of the process so they understand what is happening and what their role will be in achieving success.

Establish Communications. Develop a communication policy from the beginning so employees know where they can get information on the progress of the project.

Involve People. It's important to involve a cross-section of employees on teams that will be tasked with making recommendations. There are several reasons why you should make sure this happens. Primarily, it gives credibility to the process. It also facilitates valuable communication as team members tell their peers what is going on. The final section of this book details procedures followed by teams appointed to address priority issues.

Train People. Hold a team training session for the people who will be involved on the remediation team. They need to be told what their objectives are and how they should function as a team.

Establish Metrics. Where people are measured, people perform. Determine which people in your organization will be tasked with mitigating issues. Then give them the specific metrics they should use to measure their progress.

Reward People. Establish a reward system to recognize the work of team members. They need to know without any doubt that they are being recognized for contributions that go above and beyond their normal job descriptions.

Do Regular Reviews. Do a review of your organization's progress at regular intervals. These reviews will highlight the changes that have been made to date and will keep the organization focused on resolving any remaining issues.

Don't Get Overwhelmed! The above list may seem overwhelming—but our experience with hundreds of projects has shown that these tasks are actually easy to accomplish. It's generally a matter of deciding what needs to be done and then doing it. We've seen the process at work in a broad variety of organizations, and noted that the entire process is nonintrusive in an organization's day-to-day operations. The important thing to remember is that the results are worth the effort. PriorityPath® really works!

Chapter 4

How We're Different from Traditional Approaches

Traditional risk analysis and risk management processes are designed to do exactly as their names imply: to discover the risks that face an organization. These types of processes are typically used to help an organization meet Occupational Health and Safety Administration (OSHA) regulations, to determine financial risks, and to determine how much insurance an organization needs.

Risk Analysis

Most commonly, risk analysis techniques range from having experienced people make educated judgments about the severity of the risk to more formal, mathematical treatments, such as Fault Tree Analysis, Hazard and Operability studies, Failure Mode and Effects Analysis, Monte Carlo modeling, and many more. Each of these techniques has particular advantages, most of which apply most effectively to hardware and technical systems.

Regardless of the technique that is used, risk analysis seeks to identify specific risks—usually in isolation from each other—and to present them in a formal format. Those typical formats include tables, lists, charts, graphs, narrative reports, and cause/effect trees of various types.

More about Surveys

As mentioned, most of the risk analysis techniques work most effectively in the analysis of hardware and technical systems. Several techniques have been developed to judge the degree of risk associated with human activity; pair-wise comparison is one example.

Usually, though, analysts use some sort of checklist or survey to quantify human risks. That quantification then depends on the statistical methods or other measures used to calculate probabilities. When these methods are used with data that reflects human activity, parametric statistical approaches are commonly used—but there is significant probability that the metrics will be skewed, simply because this mathematical base is generally inappropriate or just wrong.

Chapter 4 • How We're Different from Traditional Approaches

Survey	vs.	PriorityPath®
Collects selective issues	vs.	Collects all known issues
Interpretation and tabulator bias	vs.	Rank orders all issues and paths by significance
Interrelationship of issues not considered	vs.	Considers interrelationship of related issues
Low organizational acceptance	vs.	High organizational acceptance
Questionable framework for improvement	vs.	Framework for improvement

Figure 5 Comparison of Surveys and PriorityPath® Methodology

As mentioned earlier, PriorityPath® is quite different from survey approaches; some of those differences are illustrated in Figure 5. The figure and following discussion elaborates the differences.

When a survey is prepared, the practitioner has to assemble a list of issues that he or she believes will explore the areas that are of interest to those who authorize the survey. Regardless of whether the survey preparer talks to people familiar with the survey subject, the survey contains the biases of the person who prepares it. Even the process of choosing which items will appear in the survey requires the preparer to use personal judgment—another manifestation of bias. Whenever a survey is administered, some group inevitably claims that the survey dealt with the wrong issues. This reflects one of the inherent limitations of surveys; obviously, a survey can examine only the issues that the preparer has included in the survey.

Differences in Statistical Measures

A rather wide array of statistical techniques can be used to analyze survey results; some of those include distribution statistics, measures of shape, and measures of variation.

Distribution Statistics. Distribution statistics are used to summarize the distribution of values. The first (lower) quartile represents that 25 percent of the other values are below that value. The third (upper) quartile represents that 25 percent of the other values are above that value. The inter-quartile range is the set of values between the first and third quartiles, or the middle 50 percent of all values.

Measures of central tendency are generally located near the center of the distribution of values. The arithmetic mean—or average—is the sum of the values in the set divided by the number of elements in the set. The median is defined as the middle value when the element numbers are lined up in increasing or decreasing order. The mode is the value that occurs most often in the set of numbers. In a distribution with perfect symmetry, the mean, median, and mode are the same number.

Measures of Shape. Most of the time, the distribution will be skewed away from the median. *Skew* is the measure of the lack of symmetry in the distribution of the data values. A positive skew means most of the data falls to the left of the mean and the tail of the distribution is to the right. A negative skew indicates that most of the data falls to the right of the mean, and the tail of the distribution is to the left. *Kurtosis* measures the heaviness of the tails in the distribution.

Measures of Variation. Measures of variation indicate the distribution of the values. The range is defined as the difference between the minimum (smallest) and maximum (largest) values. Deviation is defined as the distance of the measurements away from the mean. Variance is the sum of the squared deviations from the mean divided by the number of elements less one. The standard deviation is the positive square root of the variance.

Most of these techniques make the assumption that the data collected has *scalar magnitude,* a common precondition to applying many statistical methods. Immediately, the probabilities derived from these techniques will not accurately reflect the judgment of the people who were surveyed. As a consequence, surveys are often not accepted in organizations—and, consequently, there is little chance that improvements will be made on the basis of the survey.

PriorityPath® uses a different statistical approach. Instead of selecting a few items that will be included in a survey, PriorityPath® requires that the input of every participant be recorded. Every input is included in the rating instrument and is rated for relative significance using a non-parametric statistical routine. Instead of reporting only the responses to predetermined survey questions, the results of a PriorityPath® study list every issue in rank order and from every perspective of interest to the client. The relationships among those issues are shown on both a diagram and in a booklet. These

Chapter 4 • How We're Different from Traditional Approaches   39

relationships are also quantified and shown as normalized ordinal probabilities. Because of our unique process, PriorityPath® results can be used as a basis to make significant changes in organizations.

PriorityPath® Project Contrasted with a Survey

The difference between using a survey and using PriorityPath® can be seen in a project we conducted with the mining and chemical division of a large farm services company. The company used PriorityPath® at the same time that it conducted a major survey study. Both our project and the survey were focused on helping the company increase sales and profits and to be more productive.

The survey, prepared by a prestigious research firm, consisted of 75 questions and was administered to the entire workforce of approximately 6,000 people. It resulted in a 12-foot stack of report documents that the division vice president indicated was nearly useless. In fact, the interpretation of the survey results was skewed and was used to conduct a witch hunt among employees. As a result, the company experienced a major morale problem until the company abandoned the survey recommendations.

In contrast, PriorityPath® analysts gathered information in individual interviews with approximately 220 employees chosen by management to represent all parts of the company. We formatted the information we gathered and displayed it on a diagram that everyone in the company was free to examine. The results were used to resolve several outstanding issues, such as focusing efforts on securing more raw materials, revamping the retirement system (which had caused major contention among company employees for many years), and getting a production facility that had suffered a $100 million loss back into operation.

Another similar project also highlights the differences between survey results and the PriorityPath® approach to determining priorities. A survey was posted on the Internet to get the views of as many students as possible about improvements they wanted to have implemented in student services on campus. In addition, survey results were collected from approximately 65 focus groups of alumni, administrators, staff, instructors, and others. Campus officials charged a committee with responsibility to extract from the survey results the priorities of various groups on campus—for example, freshmen, graduates, and instructors.

The committee knew that the statistical means to extract such information from the data at hand was not available. The university went to work to identify best practices, and was referred to Priority Systems®. We initiated a project and formatted the survey data that had been collected into four Validation Diagrams, which were subsequently edited by several hundred people in the university community. Students, alumni, staff, administrators, and other employees of the university then rated the findings and results were produced, showing the specific priorities of 23 separate groups.

The committee used our information to provide the university administration with a statement of direction for improved student services that accommodated the priorities we had identified. Within a brief period, another major university conducted a similar study and achieved similar results. The two projects we did for the universities showed how we can translate the meaning of obscure survey results into priorities for action.

PriorityPath® and Delphi Studies

The similarities between PriorityPath® and Delphi Studies are primarily limited to methods of securing input data. Both seek the creative input of participants. However, unlike Delphi studies, the PriorityPath® approach does not limit input to experts in the field—any person who is experienced, irrespective of level of expertise, may be invited to contribute creative ideas in PriorityPath® projects. Sometimes experience in the organization is at least as valuable as expertise in identifying areas that need attention. The major difference, however, is in the methods used to determine which issues are of high priority. Delphi studies typically use a Blue Ribbon panel of experts to sort submissions, select common themes, and cycle them back to participants several times until convergence toward common themes among the expert participants is observed. While this may have some utility, there is a danger that the most creative input may be edited out by the panel simply because certain creative ideas were submitted by only one or a very few persons. The PriorityPath® approach avoids this problem by having all participants make judgments about every issue that any of the participants suggests is relevant to the mission upon which the study is focused. The PriorityPath® approach is comprehensive in that it beneficially exploits the creative thinking of all participants in both data gathering and assessment rather than limiting these considerations as does the Delphi approach.

CHAPTER 5

THE PRIORITYPATH® PROCESS

Who Can Benefit?

Our combined experience with organizations of many types over many years has shown that the greatest benefit of our process occurs in organizations that have at least one of the following characteristics:

1. Executives know they have a problem and they want to solve it—or they *sense* there is a problem, and they earnestly want to discover, analyze, and address it.
2. Executives initiate a project because they want to improve the system more quickly. They want to marshal all of the resources of the organization toward accomplishing an expanded view. When stakeholders (both inside and outside the organization) have the chance to contribute what they know about things that could improve operations and remove impediments, they get a heightened sense of ownership and personal responsibility for the success of the entire enterprise. The process of getting people involved results in improved teamwork, stronger morale, release of pent-up frustrations, removal of obstacles, improved productivity, and greater profit.
3. Executives who initiate a project are typically progressive people and early adopters. They are willing to try a different approach on the promise that they will actually see a savings in time and money, additional profits, growth, and organizational improvement.
4. Executives sometimes initiate a project to perform an organizational assessment, something that's often done by new executives who want to learn about the organization. Instead of taking the six to twelve months that are usually required to "get up to speed," we can give new executives information about the organization's critical issues within a few weeks. This includes a profile of the executive's personal priorities, which can then be compared and contrasted with those of the management team and with every other group. The same thing can be accomplished if the executive wants to perform a system audit or catalog system strengths and weaknesses, a good

precursor to projecting immediate and future needs. PriorityPath® has been used in these situations very effectively.

In addition to these four factors, we find the greatest success with executives who value the input of stakeholders—including employees and outside people who have relevant knowledge about the organization. These outside people could include customers, suppliers, financial advisors, accountant firms, consultants, investors, advisory boards, advertising agencies, the press, and, where appropriate, members of the general public. Those who most effectively use PriorityPath® act on the adage that "all of us know more than any one of us," even if that one person is the CEO or president of the organization.

Overview of the PriorityPath® Process

Priority Systems®, the exclusive provider of the PriorityPath® process, provides specialized services that help organizations identify, prioritize, and control risks, issues, deficiencies, and other factors upon which success depends. The analytical process we use has its roots in the aerospace industry.

Most risk management tools available today focus on hardware applications—but most organizational problems involve human judgments and the interactions of humans with technical components. That truth is amply illustrated by the *Challenger* and *Columbia* incidents discussed in the Introduction and Appendix E.

As increasingly complex issues and risks arise in the future, organizations will more eagerly want to assess the impact of human and human/technical factors in their organizations. We realized early the need for rigorous tools to analyze the human factor, and as a result we began a twenty-year search for a solution. That search culminated in the development of PriorityPath®. The process combines a methodology and technology to provide comparable rigor to what is generally used to analyze hardware systems—but the primary focus of our methodology and technology is to resolve issues that involve people. Our research leads us to continually refine our process, which enhances the success of the organizations with which we work.

A PriorityPath® Project: The Steps You'll Take

For purposes of illustration, we'll assume that your project relates to port security. Obviously, the same general steps apply to any problem, focus, or organization.

1. Prepare a Mission Statement

You'll develop a draft of a mission statement that will focus and set the boundaries for the analysis. The following statement is an example:

To ensure the safety and security of the port and to share responsibility among port stakeholders to prevent criminal and terrorist activities that would affect the peace, order, safety, and operations of the port.

It's critical that you write a mission statement to guide the project. The mission statement should be written by you and others in your organization, and it should reflect the specific areas on which the analysis should focus. Many organizations use a steering committee comprised of senior executives together with a small representative sample of people at lower levels in the organization. Most steering committees consist of ten or fewer people so that decisions aren't delayed by prolonged debate. Other organizations simply assign one person to be responsible for drafting the mission statement.

The example mission statement was drafted by a group of people who were familiar with the issues involved in improving port security after the terrorist attacks in New York City on September 11, 2001.

2. Gather Information

You will schedule interviews between our analysts and the people who have the appropriate knowledge about port security. We will collect information without disclosing who said what—a process that ensures quality data and protects the anonymity of contributors.

As we gather data, we'll ask people three questions about port security:

- What should we be doing that we are not doing, and why?
- What problems now exist that must be resolved if we want to accomplish the mission?
- What potential problems may be encountered as we take action to accomplish the mission?

The process of gathering information can vary. We might incorporate all available data into the analysis—including things such as recent reports about the issue(s), survey results, responses to e-mail submissions, consultants' notes, annual reports, meeting minutes, and so on. When large numbers of people are invited to contribute points of view, we might also gather information in both large and small group meetings. Regardless of whether we use individual interviews or group meetings, we use the same three questions to obtain the relevant information about issues and their impacts.

Our process is markedly different from the approaches that are normally used to gather information. With most processes, interviewers will ask respondents to talk about both areas of excellence and areas of need. The analysis that follows then focuses first on congratulating the client organization on its accomplishments, then mentions a few areas where changes may be considered. While this technique is flattering to the client, it does very little to provide strategic or tactical direction about what needs to be done. Also, the suggested direction is colored by the biases of the person who is giving the suggestion. The suggestions are usually rejected for a simple reason: they seldom reflect the thinking of the people in the organization. In contrast, we focus our information gathering on the problems, deficits, and needs identified by the people who are actually experiencing them.

There is little need to examine areas that are under control. Instead, you need to determine the hidden issues—the nature and causes of the problems that are not going away and how they are related. You need to prioritize them and suggest action that will bring them under control. Our approach lasers in on the most critical areas and provides strategies that will get rid of the stresses (even the hidden ones) that are causing problems for the organization.

Using our analysts to gather information has additional benefits. People in an organization are often reluctant to mention their own hurts, concerns, and fears to their associates—especially to executives. When outside analysts gather the information, people are usually incredibly open and honest.

3. We Construct and Approve the Validation Diagram

Using the data we gathered, our analysts create crisp statements that summarize the content of the interviews. The analysts format the information into an easy-to-use cause/effect diagram. Those who participated in the interviews get the opportunity to edit the data, a step that ensures that the content is accurate. It also ensures that the cause/effect relationships developed by the analysts are reasonable, the data is exhaustive and complete, and the language used clearly reflects what the contributors intended. Because those who are interviewed remain anonymous, this validation review is the first time participants can see what others said. During this review, participants often remember additional information, and those perspectives are added.

The major goal of our analysts at this point is to capture the intent of the people who were interviewed and to create crisp statements about every issue that was identified. We use "near quotes" so people can easily see that their contribution was captured in their own language. We've tried using computers and tape recorders during the interviews, but we found that they were disruptive to the smooth flow of information. Instead, our interviewers listen, take notes, probe for deeper understanding, and try to faithfully represent the intent of each participant. If someone cannot attend an interview, we can communicate by phone or over the Internet, though we prefer face-to-face interviews.

When we finish the interviews, we collate the responses into meaningful, brief statements that represent to the greatest degree possible every issue, problem, suggested need, risk, and barrier that each participant mentioned. These crisp statements are then organized into a Validation Diagram—a tree-like display that places each statement in a cause/effect relationship with all other issues in the database. The challenge to the analysts is to make sure that every critical statement is included, that there are few (if any) duplications, and that the cause/effect relationships are at least reasonable. If we can't establish a true cause/effect relationship for an item, we must at least show an association between higher-level and lower-level event statements within the tree-like structure of the Validation Diagram.

As mentioned, the participants are invited to edit (validate) the diagram. This not only ensures that the data is exhaustive, complete, and properly formatted, but provides a chance for participants to see the issues that their associates think are critical. Participants then talk about the most critical concerns of people in all parts of the organization, often for the first time. Typically, individual participants recognize those areas of concern within their scope of responsibility that others have identified as major issues. People frequently then return to their offices and start implementing remedies for issues they hadn't even realized were of any consequence to their associates. As a result, many issues are actually solved well before the analytical results of the analysis are available.

It's important to note that none of the information comes from the analysts—all the analysts do is connect the statements they received to similar ideas in logical sequences. Unlike usual consulting or survey approaches, our database contains no consultant bias. The resulting issues are those that the participants—not the analysts—believe are critical.

4. We Arrange for Rating (Quantification) of the Issues

After participants have validated (edited) the diagram, the information it contains is placed on a dedicated Web site located on a secure server. (If Internet access cannot be arranged, we use specially prepared rating booklets to allow participants to complete the rating activity.) Participants who use the Internet are given a secure user name and password; when they are entered, a screen appears so the person can describe his or her association with the organization: senior executive, board member, operator, planner, and so on. Instructions for rating the significance of each issue are then presented; those instructions are listed in Appendix A.

The participants are then asked to make the following judgments about each item in the database:

- How important is the issue?
- How familiar are you with the issue?
- How frequently does the issue occur, or could it occur?
- What relative level of effort would be required to fix or avoid the issue in the future?

The Quantification/Rating instrument, whether in the online or paper/pencil version, appears in a format similar to that in Figure 6.

Project Mission:

AAADA -- There is concern about policies with respect to deployment of high achievers and career underperformers. because...
(Page 3)

		Importance	Familiarity	Frequency	Remediation
AAADAA	The firm has an imperfect plan with respect to challenging the best to improve and terminate the worst.	0 1 2 3 4 5 ●	L M H ●	L M H ●	L M H ●
AAADAB	There is need for a guidebook on hiring and terminations.	0 1 2 3 4 5	L M H	L M H	L M H
AAADAC	There is a need to provide a clear career path for technical resources beyond senior consultant.	0 1 2 3 4 5	L M H	L M H	L M H
AAADAD	Some partners do not pay sufficient attention to "care and feeding" of staff.	0 1 2 3 4 5	L M H	L M H	L M H
AAADAE	The right number of partners and staff is needed in each area to meet the needs/potential of providing products and services in that area.	0 1 2 3 4 5	L M H	L M H	L M H

Next | Reset

You have completed 5 of 55 event sets.

Figure 6 Example of the Quantification/Rating Instrument

Chapter 5 • The PriorityPath® Process

We use four factors to rate the relative significance of each issue the participants identify: (1) importance, (2) familiarity (level of expertise), (3) frequency of occurrence, and (4) remediation (how much effort would be required to manage the issue). This contrasts markedly with the way that other priority-setting systems rate the relative significance of factors. Fault Tree Analysis (as noted previously, applicable only to engineering systems) uses two inputs, Mean Time Between Failures and Mean Time to Repair.

Most systems use a percentage estimate to indicate the importance of each factor. In reality, however, percentages imply a certain degree of precision that cannot be derived from a human judgment.

Force Field Analysis techniques (discussed in Chapter 6) generally consist of drawing lines; the length of the line indicates a subjective estimate of how important the factor is.

Pareto charts are used to graphically summarize and display the relative importance of the differences between groups of data.

Other statistical routines, such as pair-wise comparison and similar techniques, tend to use only one or two measures of judgments of relative importance.

While brief, these notes show that the input data used in our process is more complex and extensive than with most other priority-setting techniques.

5. We Analyze the Data and Present the Results

The participant ratings are processed using a proprietary, validated, and programmed mathematical algorithm that calculates a Strategic Event Value (SEV) for each issue/risk in the database. The SEVs are statistically normalized so they are easy to use and understand as you compare the priorities of individuals and groups.

Utilizing the results, we produce output documents (in the form of diagrams and booklets) that show the priority of every issue/risk for each reporting category as identified by the people most familiar with them—the people in your organization. We highlight the highest priority items so that both your participants and management can see *precisely* where there are similarities and differences in how they perceive high-priority issues/risks. As those differences are identified, action is taken to reconcile the mismatches. Quality solutions are created as organized task teams address the high-priority issues and integrate newly formulated remedial actions with ongoing processes.

The way we analyze data and present the results is unique to the PriorityPath® process and is proprietary to Priority Systems®. Later in this book, you'll see a brief description of the mathematical algorithm we use, as well as a summary of its development and validation.

Immediate attention should be focused on the issues that everyone agrees are high priority—but the other data is also extremely valuable. Why? Knowing where various groups differ in their rating of issues makes them manageable. It also raises two important questions: "What does someone else know that I don't know?" and "What do I know that others do not know?" Participants and management in your organization can now see where different individuals and groups rate items high or low. This information helps both your participants and management bring focus and consensus on the most critical factors that different groups believe must be addressed to accomplish the mission, in this sample case, to ensure port security.

What you'll see next (see Fig. 7) is an illustration of a single page from a report document of the sample PriorityPath® project focused on port security. Typical project reports are 25–75 pages in length. This page illustrates the usefulness of the data that is collected, processed, and subjected to rigorous, formal assessment. Even though this data was created only for this illustration, the actual information we used was contributed by experts who are familiar with conditions at a major United States port.

The numbers are normalized ordinal probabilities calculated from the judgments made by project participants using the rating instrument described above. We chose a cut-off point to show the top 20 percent of the critical issues; these numbers are bold and underlined. This follows the Pareto principle, which suggests that addressing the top 20 percent of issues will remediate as much as 80 percent of the critical problems in an organization.

In this example, we are comparing the priority concerns of the combined group with those of specialized interest groups associated with the port—such as law enforcement agencies, first responders, facility owners, port authority, and mobile transportation personnel. Note that there is only *one* area where all agree that an issue is high priority. In two other areas there is general agreement, but the issues are considered to be less important.

The numbers in the chart are Normalized Ordinal Probabilities, usually referred to as Strategic Event Values or SEVs. They provide a

Port Security

	CMBND	LAWENF	FRSRES	FACOWN	PORTAU	MOBTRA
There is concern that the Port is operating with inadequate equipment because . . .						
A tugboat is needed at the dock to push ships and barges away.	0.187	0.729	0.229	0.569	0.224	**1.000**
There is a need for more remote sensors, sniffers and cameras.	0.613	**0.975**	**0.556**	0.810	0.750	**0.942**
More high speed patrol boats are needed.	0.134	0.602	0.148	0.788	0.539	0.845
Greater cooperation is needed among the public and private agencies operating in the Port because . . .						
There is a need for enhancing a holistic "one port" perception.	0.574	0.489	0.486	0.785	0.216	0.764
Problems of individual facilities.	0.792	**0.866**	0.778	0.655	**0.901**	**0.853**
There is a lack of trust in data security and use (people will not participate).	**0.986**	**0.965**	**0.961**	**1.000**	**0.972**	**0.992**
Better understanding is needed about interrelationships among port facilities—waterway, pipelines, power lines, etc.	**0.905**	**0.947**	0.615	**0.993**	**0.986**	0.563
There is a need for continuous and effective cooperation among the local, state, federal, and private sectors.	0.500	0.771	0.342	**0.993**	0.472	**0.942**

Key: CMBND = Total Group, LAWENF = Law Enforcement, FRSRES = First Responders, FACOWN = Facility Owners, PORTAU = Port Authority, MOBTRA = Mobile Transportation.

Figure 7 Prioritized Results of the Sample Project

valid measure of the level of concern, in rank order from 1.000 (highest) to 0.001 (lowest), for each item in the database and for each of the participating groups. Items with a ranking of 0.850 and above represent approximately 20 percent of the items in each group, consistent with the Pareto principle. Because these probabilities are normalized, there is some degree of comparison possible across groups. For instance, for the item "More high speed patrol boats . . ." it is apparent that none of the groups consider the issue to be as critical as the other items that are rated above 0.850. For the item beginning "There is a lack of trust in data security . . ." it is apparent that all groups consider the item to be relatively critical. Examination of the chart can therefore provide specific information about those issues that the different groups believe need to be addressed. This mathematically valid and reliable data then becomes the basis upon which decisions can be made about priority actions that should be taken.

Separating the Critical Few from the Trivial Many

The SEVs we calculate provide a priority ranking for every issue in the database and identify the ones that your participants consider to be of high priority. In essence, this separates the "critical few from the trivial many." You don't need to address every issue that is raised; such an exercise would be prohibitively expensive, time consuming, and unnecessary. On the other hand, we prioritize the issues/risks that the knowledgeable people you have chosen to help assess your operation have identified. This enables you to focus on the areas where your people believe your organization is most vulnerable, indicating with precision where your resources can be spent most wisely. Our process dramatically helps you to measure where consensus about critical factors exists among key people and groups, a necessary prerequisite for securing commitment toward making the remedial changes that will make a poor situation good and a good situation outstanding.

In addition to a numerical reporting document that shows results as illustrated in Figure 7, we also prepare charts that show the same data in a variety of ways, making it easy for participants to see precisely where the groups agree and differ on the issues examined. A representation of these charts is shown in Appendix F.

Actions to Resolve High-Priority Issues

The final step in our analysis process is to determine the appropriate actions to resolve the high-priority issues and to implement those remedial actions. As previously noted, remediation actually starts when participants examine the database during Validation; it is reinforced and continued as results of our assessment become known. At this final stage, formal plans and actions are generated to address the most critical issues.

After participants have had the chance to reflect on the findings of the project, our personnel help participants extract the basic themes that emerge; we also provide assistance in amalgamating the findings of the project with existing plans and operations. As this kind of follow-up action is taken, we significantly increase the probability that your organization can do those things that focus all participants on accomplishing the organization's mission.

We have produced a set of instructions that describe the activities that have proven useful as theme teams have addressed priority issues identified in a PriorityPath® project. These instructions are found in Chapter 11, "Translating Findings to Action: Where to Go from Here."

Summary Statement

The analysis technique we use is a unique, comprehensive, computer-based, issues-management system. This system identifies, documents, clarifies, prioritizes, and facilitates control of the issues that if not identified and dealt with properly can inhibit or destroy what your organization is trying to do. The system focuses on critical issues and facilitates the wise use of energy and resources in high-priority areas where timely investment can make the greatest contribution towards accomplishing positive goals.

PriorityPath® Deliverables

As part of our analysis, we'll deliver the following to you:

Validation Diagram and Document. This document shows the potential and actual issues that exist in your organization in an easy-to-understand cause/effect format.

Rating Instrument (Internet). This instrument is used by participants to determine their priorities, and we use it to collect the data we need to determine priorities of each issue.

Report Documents. These display the perspectives of everyone who participates—both as individuals and as combined groups—so you can easily see the high-profile, most critical issues and how the potential issues may play into the situation.

SEV Diagram. This diagram shows the Strategic Event Values—the normalized ordinal probability numbers that show your organization's issues in degree of severity. What you see in this color-coded reporting chart is the collective perspective of the individuals and groups that participate in the interviews and ranking process.

Strategic Path Diagrams. These color-coded diagrams, one for each participating group, display only the high-profile issues from the perspective of each group. These diagrams are available in several formats to make it as easy as possible for you to identify the next steps.

Narrative Report. At the conclusion of the project, we prepare and submit a summary of the project objectives, procedures, findings, themes, recommendations, plans, and the actions you decided on.

CHAPTER 6

THE THEORY THAT MAKES IT WORK

Force Field Analysis

The theoretical construct known as Force Field Analysis, which places the forces that impinge on organizations into focus, was developed by Dr. Kurt Lewin[1] of the Massachusetts Institute of Technology. His model examines the concepts of driving forces, resisting forces, and equilibrium.

Driving forces are those forces that push an organization in a particular direction. They tend to initiate change and keep it going. Some examples of driving forces include assignment of employees, financial resources, facilities, equipment, and organizational processes.

Resisting forces are the forces that restrain or reduce the effectiveness of the driving forces. They consist of any issue or risk that inhibits progress. Known issues or risks could include economic, legal, or operational issues; government regulations; or factors such as fear, apathy, hostility, habit, and tradition. Potential issues and risks can also play a part; these would include any issue or risk that people associated with the organization believe might come up to inhibit progress—the "what-if" scenarios that organizations dread.

Equilibrium is reached when the sum of the driving forces equals the sum of the resisting forces. In other words, the pressures driving the organization toward successful accomplishment of its vision, mission, aspirations, goals, and objectives are modified or restricted by the resisting forces until equilibrium exists. Unless 100 percent success is achieved, a gap exists—current efforts are not accomplishing everything the organization initially expected. Most managers who see this gap tend to increase the strength of the driving forces—to "pour more fuel on the fire." Inevitably, though, resisting forces simultaneously gather strength.

According to Dr. Peter Senge,[2] "Well-intentioned interventions call forth responses from the system that offset the benefits of the intervention—the harder you push, the harder the system pushes back; the more effort you

---

[1] Lewin, Kurt. *Field Theory in Social Science: Selected Theoretical Papers* (D. Cartwright, editor), New York: Harper Torchbooks, 1951.
[2] Senge, Peter. *The Fifth Discipline: The Art and Practice of the Learning Organization*, 1990 (First Edition) 1994 (Paperback Edition) p. xxiii.

expend trying to improve matters, the more effort seems to be required." Dr. Stephen R. Covey[3] points out that "the Force Field model demonstrates that change can be increased or decreased by changes in the relationship between the driving and restraining forces." While both of these authors recognize the need to identify and address the two forces, they do not present a rigorous method of analyzing them.

These opposing forces are the restraining or resisting forces. When their impacts are ignored, preventable problems occur, usually with serious consequences. The ultimate result can be that progress is halted or delayed, expense and liability are increased, revenues are lost, and inefficiencies continue. And even though the company adds resources, the problems remain.

Force Field Analysis theory suggests that in addition to "pouring fuel on the fire," another, fully congruent approach should be pursued; after strengthening the driving forces (which should be done with as much energy and resources as possible), the organization should identify, analyze, and reduce the impact of resisting forces. Several techniques have been developed in an effort to accomplish exactly that, but few of them provide ways to objectively measure the impacts of resisting and driving forces. In fact, to our knowledge, measurement of the interrelationships among resisting and driving forces is not found in the literature. Most of the techniques use intuitive or graphic estimates to portray the best means of countering the resisting forces and moving forward. These systems tend to rely on the observations of a few people who make personal judgments about how each force affects the entire system.

As confirmed by Senge, planning that concentrates only on managing the driving forces can yield disappointing results. It is necessary to do more than prepare a plan, draft a budget, manage it, and expect that nothing will interrupt the projected flow of the plan. You must also discover, understand, document, analyze, and address the ever-present resisting forces so that the driving forces—which are so well conceptualized in planning and budget documents—will not be restrained. Addressing the other end of the driving force–resisting force continuum can substantially reduce the impacts of any possible risks.

While these writers (Lewin, Covey, and Senge) suggest the importance of identifying the resisting forces, they have not, as far as we have been able to ascertain, suggested a rigorous and validated process with which to do it. With the development of PriorityPath®, Priority Systems® has solved this obvious need.

---

[3] Covey, Stephen R. *The Seven Habits of Highly Effective People*, New York, NY: Simon & Schuster, 1989.

Measurement of Resisting Forces

PriorityPath® does much more than identify the driving forces—it facilitates accurate measurement of the impacts of resisting forces from the differing perspectives of all of the individuals and groups associated with your organization. It also measures the impacts of driving forces that you should be using but are missing as well as the interactive effects of the driving and resisting forces on each other and on the entire system. It then provides a practical foundation on which you can plan remedial action that will move your organization forward. It specifically illustrates how the strength of specific resisting forces can be reduced so that the opposing driving force can be unleashed and permitted to accomplish the purposes for which it was designed.

Management education programs equip managers with a variety of excellent tools for developing and implementing driving forces—so it's not surprising that goals, objectives, policies, plans, and procedures are typically formulated as driving forces. Unfortunately, little academic attention is given to quantifying the impacts of resisting forces on the driving forces. It is into this largely unknown area that Priority Systems® has made its major contribution, as demonstrated in Figure 8.

The PriorityPath® process specializes in identifying, prioritizing, and controlling critical resisting forces. It also helps organizations identify critical driving forces that aren't having the intended impact. Our process identifies known and potential problems, risks, deficiencies, and every significant issue that is preventing the organization from achieving its vision, mission, or goal

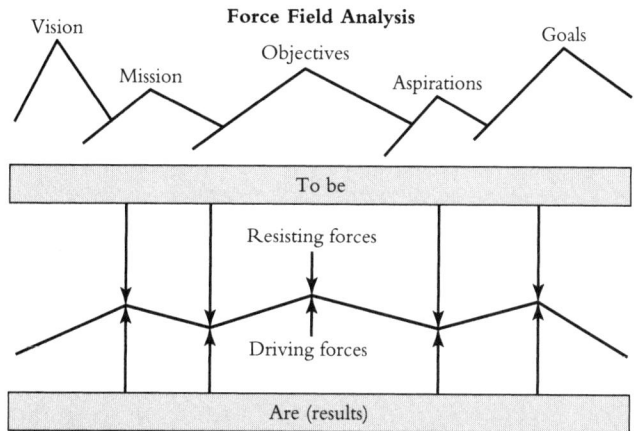

Figure 8 Schematic of Force Field Analysis

in the most efficient, effective, and timely way possible. We then format these issues in cause-and-effect sequences and analyze them, facilitate rating each issue for relative significance, calculate priorities for key individuals and groups, and initiate remediation activities. As a result, the strengths of the resisting forces are weakened and offset by focused remedial action, making it possible for the driving forces to drive the organization forward as planned. Accomplishment of missions, goals, and objectives is much more likely.

The Counterintuitive Approach

One passage in *The Fifth Discipline* by Dr. Peter M. Senge is especially relevant to the discussion of the driving force–resisting force concept, upon which PriorityPath® analysis is based. Senge recounts this experience:

> *Some years ago, I witnessed a tragic accident while on an early spring canoe trip in Maine. We had come to a small dam, and put into shore to portage around the obstacle. A second group arrived, and a young man who had been drinking decided to take his rubber raft over the dam. When the raft overturned after going over the dam, he was dumped into the freezing water. Unable to reach him, we watched in horror as he struggled desperately to swim downstream against the backwash at the base of the dam. His struggle lasted only a few minutes; then he died of hypothermia. Immediately, his limp body was sucked down into the swirling water. Seconds later, it popped up, ten yards downstream, free of the maelstrom at the base of the dam. What he had tried in vain to achieve in the last moments of his life, the current accomplished for him within seconds after his death. Ironically, it was his very struggle against the forces at the base of the dam that killed him. He didn't know that the only way out was "counterintuitive." If he had not tried to keep his head above water, but instead dived down to where the current flowed downstream, he would have survived.*
>
> *This unfortunate story illustrates the essence of the Systems perspective. Structures of which we are unaware hold us prisoner. Conversely, learning to see the structures within which we operate begins a process of freeing ourselves from previously unseen forces and ultimately mastering the ability to work with them and change them.*

PriorityPath® analysis enables organizations to escape the consequences of the resisting forces that limit success.

CHAPTER 7

DIVERGENT AND CONVERGENT THINKING:
THE MATHEMATICAL FOUNDATION

One of the characteristics of the PriorityPath® process is the anonymous interviewing and ranking that goes on—and one of the distinct benefits of that is its remarkable ability to capture and make sense of divergent thinking in an organization. The nature of almost every enterprise—whether corporate, governmental, not-for-profit, or even educational or religious—is that divergent thinking is generally suppressed. Whether it's expressly or tacitly stated, every organization has certain stated objectives (in other words, a mission statement) and certain procedures or ways the organization tries to accomplish those objectives (in other words, its organizational values). The general rule is that the more specific the objectives and the more explicit the procedures, the more effective and successful the organization will be.

Almost always, divergent thinking is a threat to well-coordinated success. You've seen it, and you've almost certainly had the experience of making a suggestion that didn't fit in with the accepted views or procedures of the organization. When that happens, the suggestion is generally stifled or simply ignored. In most organizations, a great deal of time and effort is spent trying to reign in extraneous thinking and activity to make sure that the organization's resources are funneled into the channels of endeavor that the organization officially approves.

Think about the various meetings you attend in your organization, regardless of your level of authority or participation. They're typically coordination efforts, where various people come together to "get on the same page." There's generally a vague notion that creative thinking should be encouraged; some companies give it lip service, and may even allot blocks of time to brainstorming or thinking outside the box. Some even stress the importance of raising contrary points of view. Some CEOs are even fond of saying, "Don't tell me what I think—I already know what I think. Tell me what *you* think, especially if you disagree."

Some of the best ideas have come from organizational cultures that recognize the value of innovation, that strive to get people to disagree, and that provide incentives to people for divergent thinking. That's not to say that you should simply disagree; disagreement for disagreement's sake is of little value. Unfortunately, though, few organizations—even those that encourage substantive differences and discussion—know what to do with dissent. Even in those organizations, employees tend to keep their heads down.

Generally, it takes a chief executive of unusual ability and self-confidence to truly encourage employees to express dissenting views without compromising the efficiency of the organization. And generally the only one in an organization willing to take a position contrary to the accepted line of thinking—and stick with it—is a senior executive who has a great deal of political clout or is an unusually brave individual. The political pressure of the success culture is simply too great.

So what exactly is the role of divergent thought and dissenting views? What is their value? And what do you do with them? To better understand that dynamic, let's look at the mathematical models of human interaction that underlie the PriorityPath® approach.

The Reliability and Risk Equation: P(S) + P(F) = 1

An engineer, building on pioneer risk analysis work in the aerospace industry, developed ways of applying to human behavior systematic mathematical models that are descriptive, not predictive—because human behavior is subjective, not objective. Since they account for the intricacies of human possibility, the models are very helpful in approaching the question of divergence and convergence in organizations. Over the past twenty-five years these initial findings have been further refined, and today there is sustained effort to further refine and expand the capability of the process in projects that analyze how people interact with machines as well as how people interact with each other. The early work in visionary reliability and risk methodology is a solid way to understand the flow of convergent and divergent thinking in any organization.

One of the underlying insights in this early work was drawn from the Engineering Risk Analysis literature. It is that the sum of all success factors plus the sum of all failure factors equals one—the basic formula underlying most approaches to risk analysis. In other words, all the ways that your organization might be successful combined with all the ways it might fail form one integral unit—the complete set of possible outcomes. Here's how it can be expressed mathematically, where P(S) represents the probability of success and P(F) represents the probability of failure:

$$P(S) + P(F) = 1$$

The probability of success plus the probability of failure sums to one—or, in other words, 100 percent of all activities are made up of <u>successes to any</u>

degree coupled with failures to any degree. Keep in mind that successes and failures are in a direct proportional relationship with each other; as successes increase in number, failures decrease in number (and vice versa). Any efforts to increase the probability of success, then, will suppress the probability of failure. In the same way, efforts to suppress the probability of failure will increase the probability of success.

Vote for Sally!

To better understand these concepts, imagine a political campaign. In a political campaign, of course, the desired outcome is votes. Imagine that Sally is a candidate in a municipal election, where the outcome is determined by the number of actual votes cast. Simply put, whoever gets the most number of votes wins. The possible outcomes of Sally's campaign, then, can be expressed like this:

P(Sally) + P(Other Candidates) = 1

The total of all the votes for Sally plus the total of all the votes for the other candidates equals the total of all the votes cast. In this example, it's easy to see how the statement works in direct proportion. As the percentage of total votes cast for Sally increases, the percentage of total votes cast for the other candidates decreases, and vice versa. The total of all votes remains constant (100 percent of the votes cast). However, Sally can lead campaign efforts to try to increase the percentage of votes she gets, thereby decreasing the percentage of votes the other candidates get.

To increase the success of her campaign, Sally needs to do an entire sequence of things. She needs to decide her position on issues of concern *and* determine the popularity of her positions with voters through focus groups *and* find a way to communicate her positions in a persuasive way *and* raise enough money to get her message out *and* get the endorsements of highly visible officials and agencies *and* avoid saying controversial things to the press *and* write and deliver effective speeches to key constituency groups *and* so on. That's "and" logic dominance. "And" logic is typical of planning in most organizations, and it involves the coordination and dedication of many resources toward a desired outcome.

What's important to realize is that *there is also tremendous opportunity on the other side of the plus sign.* Since there's a proportional relationship between the percentage of votes cast for Sally and the percentage of votes cast for other candidates, Sally can also increase her percentage by convincing voters *not* to vote for the other candidates.

Imagine that Sally is in the final election against Joe, and that 100 percent of the votes will be cast for either Sally or Joe. Here's how the equation of possible outcomes will look:

P(Sally) + P(Joe) = All votes (a number statistically similar to 1)

With votes for Joe representing all the votes not cast for Sally, Sally now has an opportunity to win the election in a different way. If she can reduce the number of votes Joe gets, her share of the total will automatically go up. Even if she fails to communicate popular positions that resonate with voters, if she can convince enough people that they shouldn't vote for Joe, she will win the election. (Witness the birth of negative campaigning!)

It turns out that convincing people not to vote for somebody else is actually a whole lot easier than convincing them to vote for you. Focus group after focus group in election after election bear out the almost universal truth that negative messages about a competing candidate have more impact on people's thinking and behavior than positive message ads about a given candidate's views and plans for progress. In other words, it is actually *easier* to work on the P(F) side of the equation. Why? That side of the equation doesn't emphasize "and" logic dominance, but features "or" logic dominance. Working on the P(F) side of the equation doesn't require a string of coordinated efforts—just one of many possible events. Sally can get people not to vote for Joe if she can convince them that Joe is dishonest *or* if she can convince them that Joe is not careful with money *or* if she can convince them that Joe doesn't share their values. This is "or" logic dominance in action.

Working the Averages: Playing Both Sides of the Equation

Suppose the initial implementation of your business plan yields a success rate of 60 percent. You did that as a result of determining and implementing a series of factors you know are essential to success, such as budgeting, staffing, production, maintenance, marketing, reporting, and so on. However you're not willing to settle for 60 percent success, primarily because the probability of failure would be so high—in this case, 40 percent.

Skilful Use of "and" Logic Approaches

Your immediate reaction would be to determine what additional success factors you need to add to increase the probability of success—to bring it higher than 60 percent. You might think of factors such as more reporting, more supervising, or more training, all of which require additional resources. It's back to "and" logic dominance activity; we need to do this *and* this *and* this. If you're able to add enough new success factors, you could reasonably expect that your probability of success could increase by 15 percent, making it 75 percent probable that you'd be successful. But the bad news is that even after dedicating all the additional resources to your new efforts, there's still a one in four chance (25 percent probability) that you will fail.

You're like almost everyone else; executives are conditioned to be proficient in identifying and adding success factors. They do it by using "and" logic processes. They plan diligently for success. This might work initially, and most of the time the basics are put together effectively in a short period of time. Money, time, and other resources are poured into the effort. In this case, executives are pushing Lewin's driving forces (see Chapter 6); they forget that the resisting forces are getting stronger and stronger as movement toward perfection is being made.

Multiply Successes by Using "or" Logic Approaches

So, what can be done?

Go back to the example of Sally's campaign—and remember you can take an additional approach. That approach is to devote time, energy, and resources to identifying your actual and potential failure factors and taking deliberate steps to reduce them. Remember, the failure side is characterized by "or" logic dominance; your organization might fail if it doesn't have the right people *or* it has insufficient resources *or* it does not have the policies to cope with some emergent condition *or*. . . . Single, critical events or small clusters of events can limit the effectiveness of even the best-laid plans. Because failure factors are single, usually high-profile issues or factors, they are much easier to identify and control—and are therefore less expensive to address—than the success factors on the other side of the equation. This is because success factors are usually made up of large series and sequences of factors that have to be managed together using "and" logic processes. And there is another sobering reality that enters the equation. Pouring additional time, money, and energy into efforts to secure the last few percentage points to make a venture 100 percent successful is extremely difficult and is seldom very effective. It is time consuming and usually much more expensive. It is frequently less productive than spending an equivalent amount of effort on the P(F) reduction side of the equation. Increasing pressure on the driving forces seems always to be met with equally increased pressure from the resisting forces. So we push and push against obstacles that keep shifting, focusing against us and hedging up every effort we make to move forward. We settle into plateaus, modify our vision, and let organizational lethargy dominate our thinking. We finally "get real," and end up abandoning the dream and accepting far less than we had planned and know that we probably should be achieving.

But we need not be overcome by the failure factors. Just as Senge in the story of the young man drowning observed, we can use them to refocus the energy that we will expend on improving the organization. That approach is to limit the impact of the failure factors that we face. Doing this will enhance your probability of success. If you can limit the probability of failure by another 15 percent, you'll increase your probability of success by another 15 percent. Addressing factors that could precipitate failures and controlling or removing them is identical to managing Lewin's resisting forces. If your organization has a 75 percent chance of success (but a one in four chance of failure), reducing your failure factors by another 15 percent will raise your probability of success to 90 percent.

You'll do that in ways that are complementary to but diametrically opposed to the ways you usually use to achieve success. Sadly, management can become so focused on achieving success that it hesitates to examine the factors that are limiting progress. It might be too painful or embarrassing to admit that original plans haven't materialized as hoped. And people lower in the organizational structure might clearly be able to see what is limiting success, but are usually reluctant to express their point of view. Your organization, then, needs a process where that kind of essential information can be safely gathered and where it can be used to correct the problems that, if neglected, can scuttle what your organization is trying to accomplish.

Forging ahead to add every success factor while ignoring the down side is tantamount to the cry, "Damn the torpedoes. Full speed ahead!" Addressing the resisting forces—the things that might cause failure—by identifying, analyzing, prioritizing, and neutralizing their impact is akin to the way a smart, modern military commander prepares for each encounter.

Characteristics of "and" Logic and "or" Logic: Convergence and Divergence

The pursuit of success requires that you determine and adopt the correct series and sequence of factors. In other words, you'll be successful "once you get your ducks lined up." Too often, approaches that pursue success specify what people "should be" or "should do," but they often confuse needs with wants and desires. And that often causes a consensus problem. It's difficult for people to agree on every single component, and too often it postures the executives as people who deny the stakeholders of what they consider to be genuine needs. The result? There is an increase in the psychological distance between executives and employees (and other stakeholders).

The pursuit of success is critical to securing conformance in meeting predetermined standards. Compliance with laws, regulations, and standards depends on discovering and specifying correct procedures and following them carefully. The individual elements that comprise activities designed to achieve success must also conform to the standard.

Pursuing success often leads to generalization, because a large number of elements have to be implemented in sequence before success is achieved. That enables organizations to group many elements of successful plans under well-understood conceptual frameworks, to summarize a number of activities, and to apply them without needing to specify every detail every time the activity starts. For example, programmers frequently use standard code from well-recognized code libraries to accomplish standard routines. It's not necessary to reinvent code for every element of a new project. Sometimes, however, generalizations are not understood adequately, which can lead to errors when details are obscured within the generalized idea.

Finally, the pursuit of success requires convergent thinking—the thinking pattern that necessarily accompanies a focus on meeting predetermined objectives. It makes people concentrate fully on attaining the goal. Little progress toward building an organization could happen without it. However, convergent thinking—sometimes thought of as *keeping your eye on the ball*—does little to foster the broad range of thought that is necessary to creative thinking. Too many plans that focus exclusively on the achievement of specific goals produce results that are strictly unimaginative.

The following table summarizes the foregoing argument.

"And" Logic	"Or" Logic
Convergent Thought	Divergent Thought
Sequence of Events	Single Occurrences
Conformity	Innovation
Generalizations	Specificity

Obviously, the "pursuit of success" approach to accomplishing objectives has much strength; you should implement it with as much rigor as possible. It results in specifying dimensions of safety, conformity, and opportunity—basic baseline survival characteristics. Nevertheless, it also has some weaknesses that need to be addressed.

The P(S) + P(F) = 1 formula shows that if you pursue success only, you neglect the other dimension—the avoidance of failure. When you try to limit the strength of failure factors, you increase the chances of success.

Lessons from the Civil War: Full Speed Ahead

Let's go back to Commodore Farragut, hunkered down on the deck of his ironside gunship in the heat of the battle of New Orleans. Faced with the unexpected resiliency of enemy artillery, Farragut made the calculated decision to gamble the fleet in an effort to achieve the objective. There was no way to New Orleans except downriver. They couldn't get out, and waiting for reinforcements would take too long.

Farragut had 24 warships carrying 245 guns, 19 mortar boats each containing a 13-inch mortar for high-angle fire against the forts, and 15,000 army troops. After a week of mortar fire (17,000 shells) designed to neutralize the embattlements guarding the New Orleans port had failed, Farragut made the decision simply to lead his fleet past the fully functional Confederate embattlements, take whatever fire they got, and achieve the objective, New Orleans.

"Damn the torpedoes, full speed ahead!" Weighing anchor at 2 A.M. on the morning of April 24, 1862, Farragut moved his fleet single file upriver, exchanging fire with the forts and Confederate ironclads. They lost one ship and three more were disabled, but the rest of the fleet emerged intact and leveled their nine-inch guns at the city where the hapless Confederate militia guarding the city fled without a shot.

Having formulated a sound battle plan and amassed impressive resources, Farragut put his confidence in his success campaign and blasted his way through unexpected barriers. This is the approach of most organizations to challenges or difficulties—full speed ahead. But more often than not, such reckless bravery leads to failure.

Burnside Bridges

Another example from the Civil War provides a more nuanced and enlightening study of how "and" logic and "or" logic can interact on the field of play. Later that same year at the pivotal battle of Antietam, General Ambrose P. Burnside had a battle plan that called for him to cross the Rohrback Bridge to the south of the Maryland town of Sharpsburg and engage Robert E. Lee's right flank along Harper's Ferry Road. Burnside's forces vastly outnumbered the handful of Georgia sharpshooters left to defend that position. But the Georgia volunteers were well placed on a bluff overlooking the bridge under cover of a thick canopy of trees.

Chapter 7 • Divergent and Convergent Thinking 65

Throughout the morning, division after division of Federals threw themselves at the bridge, only to be gunned down. The bridge was so narrow that only five or six men could stand abreast crossing it, and all the Georgian gunsmen had to do was fire volleys into the front line of attack as wave after wave of Union soldiers attempted to cross. Burnside redoubled his efforts, throwing more men and firepower at the point of engagement, but after three hours, he had accomplished little save the deaths of hundreds of his soldiers who bravely followed orders to cross where so many had failed before.

Finally, about 1 P.M., a small Union division broke from Burnside's IX Corps and crossed the river at a fjord a mere mile downstream. They crossed undetected, and fought their way back toward the high ground overlooking the bridge on the Confederate side of the river. At the same time, two regiments—one from Pennsylvania and the other from New York—pushed their way across the bridge. The Georgian sharpshooters were forced to split their attention, and caved to the increased pressure.

One small regiment achieved what whole divisions of infantry and artillery could not by deviating from the battle plan and going downstream. They worked on the "or" logic side of the equation.

Once across the bridge, Burnside had to delay his push toward Sharpsburg another hour as the lead division had to go back for ammunition stores that should have been brought to the front earlier. By the time the Union forces started pushing toward Lee's headquarters on the Sharpsburg heights, A.P. Hill and his Confederate reinforcements arrived from Harper's Ferry just in time to repel them.

General Burnside's failures were legion, and spanned both sides of the reliability and risk equation. He failed to sufficiently engineer the success side of the equation when he had to delay his force to bring more bullets to the front. A successful military campaign has sufficient force *and* effective lines of communication *and* supply. But more significantly, he failed to mitigate the possibility of failure when stuck with his battle plan in the face of a superior enemy position. In this instance, "Damn the torpedoes, full speed ahead!" got him nowhere. He needed divergent thinking. He needed alternatives. Instead, he spent more of his resources (men and artillery and time) and achieved a frightfully costly victory. His reputation never recovered. He had been considered by Lincoln as a replacement for McClellan at the head of the whole Army of the Potomac on several occasions before Antietam, but never after. The bridge itself has forever since been known as Burnside Bridge because of the foolishly high price in blood Burnside paid to attain it.

Burnside also failed to work on the "or" logic side of the equation when he failed to deploy scouts or cavalry to watch their left flank once they had achieved the other side of the river. Scouts could have alerted him that A.P. Hill's reinforcements were on their way, and Burnside could have sought cover. Instead, they pursued their success objective—closing in on Sharpsburg from the south—without any thought to how exposed they were to attack from behind.

For Burnside, the equation might read:

P (more men and gunpower) + P (disadvantageous tactical position + lack of intelligence) = 1 (the totality of engagements in the battle)

It's hard to overestimate how freeing it can be to really understand the true purposes of convergent and divergent thinking and how to make use of both. The PriorityPath® System captures divergent thinking because of its anonymous mining of company views and attitudes and then subjects it to consensus scrutiny through rank ordering.

The problem with most organizations is that their "Burnside Bridges" are hidden from view. The PriorityPath® system helps identify your Burnside Bridges and provides a way to incorporate new ideas into the main thrust of your organization.

CHAPTER 8

WHO—AND HOW—WE'VE HELPED

The breadth of clients we have served and the topics we have analyzed show beyond any doubt that there is a real need for legitimate analytical tools capable of handling the human dimension—and that there is great power in those tools. PriorityPath® would not be an appropriate way to test equipment in a laboratory; conversely, methods of testing laboratory equipment would not be appropriate for analyzing the involvement of people within an organization. Simply, the tools required for performing the two different types of assessment are different.

Analysts should use tools that are appropriate to the task. While data about hardware systems are often included in a PriorityPath® analysis, the focus of the analysis is always the interactions among humans and among humans and machines. An analysis that uses only hardware-related tools to analyze any aspect of human activity will be misleading. PriorityPath® is appropriate in most areas where people are involved in useful activities.

Applications of PriorityPath® have been successful in many venues; some of those include:

- Organizational assessment and restructuring
- Strategic planning
- Resource prioritization
- New executive orientation to organizational needs
- Cultural awareness
- Alignment of organizations
- Mergers and acquisitions
- Due diligence
- Project design and management
- Improved efficiency/effectiveness
- Policy analysis, development, and implementation
- Frameworks for new/revised government regulations and legislation
- Business plans
- Performance audits
- Alignment of human capital
- Downsizing

- Performance improvement
- Conflict resolution
- Reengineering, empowerment
- Operations review
- Maintenance
- Total loss management
- Industrial plant startup
- Incident prevention
- Training
- Safety (OSHA) standards
- Workforce planning
- Provision of priority services
- Outsourcing
- Student achievement/school administration
- Cost containment/revenue enhancement
- Failure avoidance
- Environmental management
- Security and high-profile threats

PriorityPath® makes sure that decisions are based on the informed judgments of people who know the most about the most critical issues in the organization. We provide access to the intelligence and information that helps leaders consider the judgments of their associates, then make the best possible decisions. We capture all known and potential issues and risks perceived by the most important stakeholders associated with the organization—then we document, analyze, prioritize, and present those issues and risks in an action-oriented way so the organization can resolve them. Our process allows management access to the best and highest quality information available, which results in the best possible resolution to the issues.

One important hallmark of the PriorityPath® process is its nonthreatening nature. Stakeholders with strong beliefs and perceptions see the issues and concerns presented without attributing individual names to the judgments—and they also see the aggregate judgments of all included stakeholders. The result is a statement of group priorities that is independent of individual bias. Our experience with hundreds of analysis projects has shown that stakeholders accept the statements of group consensus that they have helped formulate. In those cases where lack of alignment becomes apparent, we are able to document and display the specific reasons for divergent views; we then present these to management—and to all stakeholders—so the issues can be resolved.

Appendix D describes a number of different projects we have conducted. The following accounts discuss a few projects with organizations we have helped. They demonstrate the agility of the process and show that the process can be applied to a broad variety of situations.

G8 Summit: Security Planning—Canada

Background

Held periodically throughout the world, meetings of international heads of state have a history of attracting protestors. Violent street protests marked the meeting of the 1999 World Trade Organization in Seattle; as many as 200 members of the National Guard and 300 state troopers were assigned to provide backup services to the police. WTO delegates had expected protests, but nothing like the storm that hit Seattle when at least 40,000 activists took to the streets. Some 5,000 protesters confronted police, and a handful launched an assault on the downtown business area, shattering windows everywhere. The protest became a major distraction to those who attended.

In April 2001, a Summit of the Americas was held in Quebec City, Canada. Before the summit opened, militant protestors broke through the three-meter-high chain-link fence and confronted the riot police in a successful bid to disrupt the opening ceremony, which subsequently was delayed by more than an hour. In order to protect the heads of state and other officials, riot police had to fire rubber bullets and tear gas at demonstrators.

Several months later, the July 2001 G8 Summit in Genoa, Italy, attracted 2,000 delegates and 150,000 protesters. There were several days of loud street protests and bloody clashes with police; one protester was killed and many were injured.

Problem

Due to the history of violence, preparations for security at the 2002 Summit held near Banff, Canada, would be critical. The meeting was to be attended by leaders of the world's major industrial democracies: Canada, France, Germany, Italy, Japan, Russia, the United Kingdom, and the United States. Leaders from several African nations were also invited to attend. Because of what had happened at earlier conferences, significant emphasis needed to be placed on physical security.

Procedure

The G8 Security Planning Team consisted of key individuals from two professional security agencies—one a national security agency and the other from Calgary. They jointly were in charge of coordinating security planning for the event. The Planning Team used the PriorityPath® process to make sure that every factor necessary to provide security was included in the plan and that every potential risk, problem, barrier, and inhibitor was appropriately addressed.

Responsibility for directing the security planning process was shared by two senior people, one from each of the two supporting organizations who were co-equal in power and authority; each had major responsibility for specifically designated areas. Initial planning included estimating how many resources would be needed and how much manpower would be required. The team also prepared by assessing threats and categorizing the strategic importance of each component of the security plan.

We interviewed key stakeholders representing senior management and staff members of the local and national security and governmental agencies, all members of the planning team, and selected public representatives. During individual interviews, each participant contributed his or her knowledge about issues he or she considered to be critical to maintaining security at the G8 Summit. We then printed the contributions of all participants on a large cause/effect diagram, and the participants edited the statements. During the editing session, participants were able to examine the concerns of their associates. Managers were able to see this preliminary information well before we distributed the final results, and they were subsequently able to remedy many problems early in the process—a phenomenon unique to the PriorityPath® process. We've found that stakeholders often want to resolve issues in their domain as soon as they know about them—and they are especially concerned that problems in their area not be considered high-priority issues by other participants. Where critical issues are concerned, no one wants to answer questions like "Who is responsible for this?" and "Why didn't we know about this and get it fixed earlier?"

We analyzed the data and presented priorities for the combined group, which consisted of all participating stakeholders, members of the local and national police services, members of the planning team, and a group of people who had previous experience in planning or operating a major event protection plan. The planning team members were particularly interested in finding out where there were differences in priorities among their own team members. Consequently, priority profiles were prepared showing the priorities of the two co-leaders of the planning team.

The results were revealing; there were significant differences among members of the groups. There were also significant differences in emphasis on many critical issues between the two leaders of the joint planning team. Because these differences were highlighted, the two leaders were able to recognize and reconcile differing points of view. If these differences had not been identified and addressed, catastrophic events would have been more likely to occur.

During reporting sessions, it was obvious that many of the high-priority issues had already been recognized, and corrective actions had already begun. But just three weeks earlier—before the PriorityPath® project started—no one was aware that these same issues were of any concern to anyone. It was during the initial review of the cause/effect diagram that participants learned that the issues were of concern to their colleagues and they began to take remedial action.

Outcome

The G8 Summit was characterized by only one arrest. No fences were breached, no windows were broken, and no cars were towed. This enviable record stands in sharp contrast to other meetings of international leaders held in other parts of the world. Members of the planning team told us that we "helped focus cooperative efforts towards the resolution of several critical problem areas. [Our] efforts in assisting the planning team to identify and rank-order priorities, highly relevant and important to the success of the overall Summit, was of great utility."

Privatization of Electricity Market—New Zealand

Background

Legislation in 1990 had enabled deregulation of the New Zealand electricity industry, but although a market program had been introduced, little progress toward implementing the program had occurred. In the summer of 1994, the New Zealand government reconstituted an agency to try again to implement the deregulation legislation. A new Wholesale Electricity Market Development Group (WEMDG) was appointed. The group consisted of a chairman who had previously served as deputy minister of several government departments; representatives of the Energy Department and other departments; politicians; and other representatives of production, distribution, and consumer interests.

Problem

WEMDG initiated four programs simultaneously to identify and remove the roadblocks that had prevented the effective operation of the market program that had been initiated four years earlier. The attorney general's department examined legal and liability issues, and a major British consulting firm in the field of economics did an in-depth review of the financial aspects of the deregulated industry. Public meetings were held throughout New Zealand; both specific interest groups and the general populace were invited to attend. Finally, Priority Systems® was engaged to identify and present the critical issues in cause/effect sequences and to obtain rank-ordered priorities for each of the interest groups.

Procedure

We conducted interviews with high-profile government and department executives in virtually every department of the New Zealand government, opposition members, representatives of every major industry in the country, all of the agencies involved in production and distribution of electricity in New Zealand, wholesale electricity purveyors, major industrial users, environmental organizations, the press, and a major economics consulting firm from London, as well as similar agencies in the United Kingdom, Germany, and Norway and some New Zealand residents. The information we collected in interviews included perceptions of why the plan hadn't worked over the four previous years, as well as suggestions about what actions should be taken. We also got input from deregulation experts in Australia, Great Britain, and Norway. Finally, we interviewed a variety of experts from around the world who were working in New Zealand to help the program become fully operational. These experts contributed their judgments about critical factors they knew needed to be addressed.

The resulting database included virtually all of the critical issues identified in each of the other three reviews. One of the members of the review group noted that results were not only valuable, but immediately actionable. While WEMDG had access to other independent recommendations from legal and industry experts, the output from the PriorityPath® analysis proved to be critical to their success. The priorities of key individuals and groups were reported, including the priorities of producers, users, on-site managers, and independent experts.

Outcome

We delivered the priorities to members of WEMDG, who also considered the expert advice they had received from the other three reviews and moved immediately to determine the changes needed to implement the deregulation regulations. The priorities of participating groups presented in project reports allowed them to consider the probable impacts of suggested changes on the entire community of interests. With this intelligence in hand, they generated modifications to existing regulations and practices. The result was that within four months after completion of our project, the market was functional. The four-year delay that preceded our work was ended. Opposition by a major industry sector, which had contributed toward major delays in the privatization process, was neutralized by actions guided by output from the PriorityPath® analysis. As a result, the New Zealand deregulation system has been used in many locations around the world as a model for establishing successful privatized electricity markets.

Energy Services

Background

During the first year of operation, the president of a new energy services company completed the acquisition of five smaller service companies. At that point, the CEO realized that he was working with five separate corporate cultures. Prior to the acquisitions, the heads of the five new divisions had been owner/presidents—and they made it clear by their actions that they were determined to retain the procedures, objectives, corporate culture, and routines of their individual, independent firms.

Problem

The president, who had experienced the benefits of PriorityPath® on two earlier projects, determined that he would try to develop an integrated culture and unify the recently acquired companies using our process. He charged us with an important challenge; he believed that the benefits he had seen in previous projects would be multiplied if we could do our analysis in a shorter time frame. As a result we worked with the president to design a quality analysis that could be done quickly.

Schedule

We started the project on a Monday, and gathered information in several locations within a 200-mile radius of company headquarters. We put short statements of critical issues on a cause/effect diagram, which was edited by the company president and his human resource specialist before the end of the week. On the following Monday morning, we presented the data to participants and invited them to rate the significance of the issues on the Internet rating instrument that same morning. We took the data from the Internet, processed it immediately, and presented the results that afternoon.

During the rest of that day and the next, meetings were held to initiate remediation activities. The entire analysis was completed in two weeks!

The speed of this project was made possible by the excellent cooperation of the organization and its officers. Both the client and our personnel were committed to providing the project deliverables in the short time specified.

Outcome

Armed with nearly instant results, the president worked with the Priority Systems® facilitators to examine the meaning of the priorities selected by project participants. They were able to clearly see the differences in perspectives among the five participating divisions, the differences among senior executives, and the differences and similarities of priorities that each senior officer had with the president.

The results led directly to the rapid development of an integrated corporate culture. The analysis showed that each of the five acquired companies had unique and positive cultural practices that needed to be retained and shared with the others. Disagreements were almost instantly overcome.

As executives came to see that they could improve the viability of their division by integrating more completely with the other divisions, all recognized the interconnectedness of the divisions. In one dramatic instance, the company avoided an additional, expensive acquisition of a high-level engineering firm that one division wanted when the key stakeholders realized the true nature of the problem that needed to be solved. Management discovered that the expertise one division wanted to acquire was already resident in one of the other divisions. Instead of making the expensive acquisition, the company initiated an internal charging system that resulted in more sharing of expertise and resources among the five constituent entities. The company increased its market share, avoided unnecessary debt, and significantly improved cooperation and communications among its divisions.

Strategic Planning—A Canadian Province

Problem

The existing strategic plan upon which the policies of a Canadian provincial government were based needed to be updated, extended, and improved. Key government personnel made the judgment that reissuing the plan annually with few modifications as had been the practice for several years was not capturing the emerging needs of constituents and was limiting creative and imaginative exploration of new areas that were needed in provincial government programs.

Chapter 8 • Who—And How—We've Helped   75

Procedure

We gathered the perceptions of critical factors and needs held by members of cabinet, their deputy ministers, and elected members of the legislative assembly in group meetings and in individual interviews. As is our usual practice, we printed the information they contributed in the cause/effect Validation Diagram that characterizes PriorityPath® analysis. The participants reviewed, modified, and ratified the information and, using the Internet, rated it for relative significance. All participants received reports that clearly showed the differing priorities of each participating group; as a result, six major themes with supporting details were identified. These results were used to focus strategic planning efforts and were incorporated into the subsequent draft of the Provincial Strategic Plan.

The data we gathered did not duplicate planning that was already being done. Instead, the analysis process accepted the generic plan that was already in place, but emphasized what the participants determined to be additional areas that needed to be included in the plan. The analysis also focused attention on current problems, barriers, and deficiencies. Finally, it highlighted conditions that participants needed to anticipate and directed preemptive attention upon critical areas so the government could address and prevent emerging issues from becoming problems.

As a result, both elected and appointed officials enthusiastically supported the process for revising the provincial government's strategic plan.

Outcome

The plan was subsequently rewritten, addressing the critical issues identified in the analysis. This made the strategic plan more robust, realistic, and practical. The plan ultimately included the perceptions of the people who are responsible for implementation—a feature that is frequently missed when an individual, small group, or consultant writes a strategic plan in isolation. Our process creates much more buy-in than is usually given to strategic plans and has proved to be an excellent platform from which to launch new initiatives.

Electronics Manufacturing

Problem

A major international electronics manufacturing firm faced multiple issues. The firm had problems with the planning, production, and sales of television production equipment. It also had difficulties with the design, production, and distribution of television sets for the North and South American markets. Finally, it faced challenges servicing a partner firm in distributing innovative programs and equipment for the burgeoning home computer industry.

Procedure

The firm decided to use the Priority Systems® process to address all three issues. One project sought to determine if it was viable to create a center of excellence for the manufacturing of TV chassis in the Americas. Another examined the best way to introduce new products to a worldwide market. A third project examined processes for integrating a recently acquired company into the structure and culture of the parent company.

Outcome

The first PriorityPath® project identified the need for a single center of excellence to serve the entire North and South American markets. Creating the single center shortened the decision-making process and enabled the company to produce TV chassis much more rapidly, even during severe worldwide shortages of component parts. The design process and delivery time of new TV platforms throughout the Americas was also accelerated; the design cycle for introducing new television sets was reduced from a year to seven months. Finally, the company saved money by modeling new products with improved design software technology before physical models were prepared.

The second PriorityPath® project—which involved introducing Web TV, digital TV, and commercial television sets to the market—found that the internal sourcing of parts could be improved. It also identified the need to train engineers on the product development process. Analysis results demonstrated that the Web TV division should be moved closer to the organization that eventually purchased it. It also established the need to locate the Digital TV division next to company laboratories and to locate the Commercial TV division closer to corporate headquarters.

A third project involved the manufacture of broadcast television systems. The firm had production facilities in Salt Lake City, San Jose, Simi Valley, and New York, and also had affiliations with three production facilities in Europe. Because this particular division had been acquired from another company, the degree of cooperation was not high among executives from the original company with more recently appointed senior executives who were more loyal to the client firm.

The problem they faced was a continuing pattern of major losses. The new owners believed that they were not receiving key information that they needed. The management style of the new owners was different from that of the previous owners. Consequently, a number of changes among key executives had taken place. To further complicate issues, projects were being rushed to market before adequate development had occurred, with the result that there were a great number of "in-the-field retro-fixes" accompanied by great dissatisfaction among clients. At the same time, the practice that had formerly been followed of paying large bonuses to sales executives was continuing, thereby exacerbating the losses that the company was incurring. The company was losing millions of dollars per year and had no indication that conditions were improving.

The analysis we performed exposed details with respect to each of these and other matters that were contributing to company losses. Some company executives were concerned and there were some changes made at the senior staff level. When company executives in Europe saw the results of the project, they moved rapidly. A change was made at the senior level and those who were perpetuating retention of practices that had existed in the previous company were either reassigned or dismissed. The manager of the Salt Lake City facility was made responsible for all American operations. He reported directly to a senior manager at the European headquarters. This new management team implemented programs that addressed the priorities that our analysis had revealed. The company became profitable and has since been sold to another firm.

Participants in the project told us that they have never seen a more effective conflict resolution process than PriorityPath®.

Test Instrument Manufacturing

Another project was conducted with a major U.S. electronics firm that develops, produces, markets, and services electronic equipment used in the production of aeronautics instruments and test equipment for the mobile telephone production industry.

The purpose of the contract with Priority Systems® was to secure better integration of the various segments of the company. The parent U.S. firm had recently acquired the Test Instruments Division of a major manufacturer in England. At the time, the U.S. and British segments of the company were continuing to operate much as they did before the acquisition occurred.

Project activities included interviews of key executives in the United States, England, and Scotland. Sales and corporate development personnel located in Japan, Germany, and France, as well as in England and the United States, were also interviewed. The mission statement was as follows:

> To energize and ensure financial success of the Company by working together and with our customers to create solutions for the world of communications.

Approximately 250 persons were interviewed, some individually and some in small groups. A database diagram containing issues that participants felt were critical to attaining the mission was produced and edited by groups of participants. The items were rated for relative significance and criticality via the Internet. Results in the form of reporting charts and documents were produced and presented in meetings to all participants.

The judgments of the seven senior managers, located in Great Britain and the United States, were presented individually to each manager. An analysis was also made of the priorities of all of the managers taken as a group. Priority Systems® personnel moderated a meeting where the executives came together to compare their individual perceptions of most critical concerns with each other and with the priorities of the group as a whole. From this meeting a plan for achieving better integration of systems within all parts of the company was formulated. The result has been that the company now confronts challenges in a more cohesive manner than was possible when they were such disparate entities.

That project resulted in several important findings. The number one issue was the lack of employee knowledge about the vision and direction of the organization; the CEO thought he had communicated the vision and direction clearly, but found that more communication was necessary. He immediately embarked on a communication campaign to educate all employees about the vision and direction of the company, which included face-to-face meetings and phone conferences via satellite facilities. The second issue involved managing people. Employee teams were organized to address internal communications, compensation, recruitment, training, and development. As a result, the number of communication programs was increased, compensation packages were modified, recruitment was supplemented by an offshore hiring program, and more specialized training was introduced to meet specific needs we had identified. Another team focused on the product development process. New product development projects were not being completed in a timely manner, so the company hired a VP of Product Development, and new product development teams were tasked with specific projects. As a result, new products were launched on a much tighter schedule.

To sum up, the changes that were initiated by our project caused the company to achieve alignment and helped it become more attractive to investors and other stakeholders.

Sydney Water Board—Australia

Problem

Montgomery Watson Harza (MWH), an engineering firm that specializes in providing culinary water and treating waste water in many nations, was invited to submit a bid on a multibillion-dollar contract to clean up Sydney Harbor—one of the world's largest, busiest, and most scenic harbors. The firm had used the PriorityPath® process on several occasions, and decided to emphasize the benefits that could be derived from the process as a competitive edge feature in their proposal. Bid proposals were submitted by several world-class contractors, but according to the team that selected the winning contractor, inclusion of the PriorityPath® process in the bid documents was the determining factor in awarding the contract to MWH.

Input into the database for determining priorities for cleaning Sydney Harbor was received from many government departments, including Finance, Judicial, Members of Parliament (including the Opposition), Environment, Policy, and Public Works. Sydney city officials were involved. Contact was made with multiple organizations that had a specific interest in the Clean Waterways project. These included Beach Watch, Greenpeace, Surfers of the World, Friends of the Earth, and several others. Government ministers and leaders of the opposition were involved as were representatives from neighboring municipalities. The project parameters included providing assurances to government that the $2 billion allocated for the project was used in productive ways.

Procedure

Over the course of several years, the PriorityPath® process was used by MWH in several projects involving not only harbor cleanup efforts, but the improvement of operations in several inland and ocean outfall waste treatment plants. We conducted interviews with representatives of all of the groups involved in each of the projects, including people from the plant itself, government oversight departments, commercial interests, and environmental watchdog groups, as well as executives of the agency charged with responsibility for providing culinary water and treating waste water in the city and surrounding area.

Outcome

These projects proved to be very successful. One plant used the process to focus its employees and personnel from the engineering company on critical technical and managerial areas that needed to be improved. Work on the plant started immediately and was finished long before similar work could even begin in a sister plant that initiated an improvement program at the same time without the benefit of PriorityPath®.

Another project at the largest inland waste water treatment facility in the system involved managers, operators, maintenance personnel, and significant outside people who represented external managers, regulatory agencies, and the public. The results were used to revise current operating procedures, improve maintenance routines, secure better access to supplies and parts, modify management methods, and solve a variety of other issues that the Water Board deemed crucial to success.

The results were impressive. The quality of discharged effluent was raised to acceptable Australian environmental standards. The project also resulted in the repair of a methane burner that had been inoperable for the previous seven years. Plant personnel also used creative methods to clean a plugged digester that had not been functioning for many months; earlier attempts to have the unit cleaned had failed due to a lack of funding, but our process helped employees find in a creative way the resources necessary to make the repairs. Without the direction and identification of critical priorities provided by the PriorityPath® project, the plant probably would have continued its past practices—and the improvements would not have been made.

At the North Head Sewage Treatment Plant, which releases effluent to the ocean (the largest plant operated by the Sydney Water Board), the mission of our analysis was to ensure that no pollution traceable to the North Head Plant would foul the nearby scenic beaches during the just-ending summer season. Prior to the commencement of our contract, MWH had commissioned a subsidiary firm to optimize the operation of the North Head and several other Sydney Sewage Treatment plants. As we interviewed the lead MWH person at North Head about his concerns and difficulties in carrying his technical agenda for optimizing operations forward, he recounted the reluctance of plant personnel to cooperate, the denial that anything could be done, the resistance to American engineers, and so on. At the conclusion of our analysis, it was apparent to the entire staff that the employees and managers were indeed preventing excellent operation by resisting the expertise that MWH had placed on site. Recognizing this major problem, immediate changes occurred. For example, following the morning on which the analysis was reported, and during which it was agreed that "Management By Walking Around" was perceived to be necessary but was lacking, several senior managers could not be found. They were, some for the first time, touring the plant to confirm whether the priorities of the employees as reported in the PriorityPath® project report were indeed true. Necessary remedial action was initiated immediately, with the result that the primary treatment plant—which had been designed to remove 40 percent of suspended solids—increased its output from 18 to 38 percent within a very short period of time. The result was that in the following summer season, for the first time in many years, there was no fouling of the nearby beaches nor the accumulation of any grease balls or other environmentally unfriendly output traceable to the North Head Plant. The manager from MWH amalgamated the recommendations he had formulated with the priorities that had emerged from the PriorityPath® analysis. Acceptance of recommendations now occurred without objection. This was in stark contrast to the experience of his colleagues working in other plants where our analysis had not been completed. They continued to be mired in interpersonal differences, organizational politics, and animosities that so often limit effective action.

Hong Kong Tunnel

Problem

Montgomery Watson Harza also used the PriorityPath® process in a project they managed in Hong Kong. Construction of a large sewage drainage tunnel under the city and harbor was three years behind schedule; the tunnel was designed to carry waste water to the world's largest waste water treatment facility, which is located on an island in the harbor. The governmental agency responsible for the project had extended deadlines for completion several times and was insisting that the entire project be completed in the ensuing eighteen months. Failure to meet the latest deadline would result in major financial penalties to the contractors. Montgomery Watson Harza was engaged to overcome problems encountered by another firm that had left the project and it needed help to identify and remove the barriers to completing the tunnel.

Procedure

PriorityPath® was employed to determine the critical impediments MWH and the other contractors would face in completing the tunnel, commissioning it, and placing the entire new system in operation in compliance with the extended schedule. We gathered information from all affected stakeholders, including the managing contractor, a consulting firm, the boring contractors, and governmental agency personnel.

Outcome

We identified priority actions for moving forward, and secured agreement for resolving each critical issue. The process led to greater understanding of the technical and management problems among all of the participating groups. The project had suffered from major misunderstandings about some of the engineering aspects of the tunnel and about having access to proper materials. When the situation was finally understood by the engineering contractors, they were able to communicate solutions to the client, and all major concerns were resolved. Initially, there had been great suspicion; as a result of our process, the firm generated a unified approach and the project was successfully completed approximately ten months before the deadline.

CHAPTER 9

CONCLUSION

Plenty of people still think that Admiral Farragut had the right approach for confronting problems that are easily overcome: *"Damn the torpedoes, Full speed ahead!"* But when immediate action may produce unknown, potentially disastrous consequences, you're much better off to fall back and regroup by meeting with the most knowledgeable people available. You should examine every possible approach to the threat—then, after fully considering all relevant factors, inhibitors, and options, decide which strategy promises the most positive results.

Opening Organizational Eyes

The PriorityPath® process opens organizational eyes. We've learned that critical information often remains hidden in the minds of people throughout the organization. With our process, that information is suddenly displayed for everyone who needs to know it. Also, the information is displayed in ways that protect participants but reveal where differences in vision are compromising success. In other words, our process gives you a clear overview of the institutional "elephant." The voices of all participants in the enterprise are documented, prioritized, and acted on. Participants are given visibility. The probability of success is greatly increased.

Successful organizations need to be doing exactly that in today's economic climate. PriorityPath® provides a proven way for it to happen—economically, swiftly, reliably, and comprehensively.

Contacting Priority Systems®

You can get in touch with us for an estimate of our services on our Web site at **www.prioritysystems.net.** Most of our projects commence after one of our analysts has met with a prospective client to review philosophy, background, processes, and expectations and to discuss the scope of a specific project.

We start by preparing a tentative mission statement with your input; then, our analyst develops a formal proposal that includes project costs. The project can then usually start within a short period of time. The time it will take to complete a project varies from a minimum of two weeks to an average of nine weeks, depending on travel requirements, availability of participants, and the urgency you feel about the areas of focus that will be pursued in the project.

If your project is smaller in scope or your budget will not allow our team to do your analysis, consider conducting your own project. Part 2 of this book shows you how.

PART 2
ANOTHER OPTION

Chapter 10

The Abacus Version of the PriorityPath® Process

You've probably seen an abacus—or at least a picture of one—even if you haven't used one. An *abacus* is a frame that holds parallel rods within it. The parallel rods are strung with movable beads that are used as counters. Simply, it's a math device. The abacus has been in continuous use in the Middle and Far East for centuries as a basic calculation instrument. While an abacus won't give you output as comprehensive as even the most basic handheld electronic calculator, it does produce more limited but rapid results that are in some ways comparable to those of more sophisticated machines.

When you use the full PriorityPath® process, you'll get a comprehensive analysis of your organization's priorities with the same kind of precision you expect from the best electronic calculating computers. But we know that a full PriorityPath® analysis program may be beyond the budget of smaller organizations—or that the issues that need to be examined might be very narrow in focus, even in a large organization. Your organization might need an immediate, independent, cost-effective way to determine priorities.

In that case, you can do a limited program yourself—much like using an abacus instead of a calculator. You'll still get reliable results that can be used to bring about effective change and improvement, without depleting the budget for the latest "handheld." Appropriately, we call it the *Abacus Version of PriorityPath®*.

With the Abacus Version, you'll do only the first phases of a full PriorityPath® project: determine a mission, analyze it, place its elements in a concise diagram, identify priorities in a simplified way, and provide strategic direction. While not as comprehensive as the full PriorityPath® process, the Abacus Version enables your organization to quickly see exactly where different parts of your organization believe action should be taken. It also equips senior managers with information about the priorities of each group in your organization. Because you involve staff at every level, people are motivated to overcome barriers, and the attention of everyone in the organization is focused on accomplishing collective goals. The process itself institutionalizes ongoing commitment toward sustainable system improvement.

Get Started by Getting Buy-In

To begin with, make sure the senior officers in your organization know there is an issue—or set of issues—that need attention, and that they are willing to focus on those issues with enough commitment to come up with the priority actions. Your organization's issue might be related to organizational structure, cost containment, improving the quality of products or services, producing a strategic plan, or any other high-profile area of interest. Regardless of the issue, make sure you have buy-in from the senior executives. No matter how important the issue, nothing will happen until the senior executives are committed to making something happen.

Draft a Mission Statement

Once you've identified the issue you're going to address, write a draft of your organization's mission statement that focuses attention on the issue. The mission statement should be a clear, crisp expression of intent that captures the direction your organization intends to go.

In most cases, the mission statement will be directed toward accomplishing some specific part of your organization's full mission. If you want to examine the *full* mission of your organization, you'll probably want to use our analysts to do a more comprehensive approach to setting priorities through a full PriorityPath® project.

Engage the Project Leader

The first task of the project leader is to refine the mission statement, making sure that its language engages all the participants. This is important because the entire analysis will be focused on accomplishing the direction that is set by the mission statement.

Next, the project leader gets the support of senior leaders and arranges for participation from a cross-section of the groups whose priorities will be analyzed in the Abacus project. The project leader is the one who will tell participants about the nature of the project and who will consider any suggestions from those groups about carrying the project forward.

Form a Steering Committee

Identify which groups will provide perspectives and judgments for your project, then ask a representative from each group to serve as a member of a steering committee. Generally, the steering committee consists of a project leader who is a senior officer of your organization, along with representatives from

Chapter 10 • The Abacus Version of the PriorityPath® Process

your board of directors (if you have one), senior management staff, middle managers, and front-line personnel. If you'll be considering priorities of outside groups, you should also invite a representative from each of these groups to participate on the steering committee.

Make every effort to keep the size of the steering committee small—we've found that a maximum of seven people is ideal.

The project leader calls a meeting of the steering committee to explain the scientific and philosophical reasons for doing the project (the initial presentation should be based on the information in Chapters 6 and 7) and to present the mission statement. This is where members of the steering committee can give input about the mission statement. Following thorough discussion, the steering committee will adopt the revised mission statement—understanding that the rest of the Abacus project will explore and finally determine the best possible way to achieve the mission they have adopted.

Select Representatives to Participate

The project leader and steering committee will then select representatives from each stakeholder group who will be invited to participate in the project. You'll want to limit the number of participants to the size of your meeting room. Most Abacus projects use a participant group of fewer than thirty, though there can be more in some cases.

The project leader will arrange for all the participants to meet. Each person should be personally invited and should receive a brief written statement that orients them to the project as well as a brief description of the factors that led to the formulation of the mission statement. Tell participants that the meeting will focus on accomplishing the mission as it is outlined in the mission statement. With the mission statement in mind, explain that each person should come to the meeting ready to give thoughtful answers to three basic questions (identical to those used for a full PriorityPath® project):

- What should we be doing that we are not doing now? Why? Why not?
- What problems now exist that must be solved if we are to accomplish the mission?
- What potential problems could be encountered when we try to accomplish the mission?

Assign someone to record each person's response in concise, crisp, clear statements. If necessary, you can get the answers to these questions in interviews, small group meetings, or telephone conversations; by examining relevant documentation; through e-mail; or in some other creative way.

Prepare a Cause/Effect Diagram

Once each participant has had a chance to respond, the project leader with appropriate assistance will then do the most labor-intensive and critical part of the analysis: collating all the responses and formulating them into a cause/effect tree-like diagram. Our experience has shown that the best way to start is by capturing each specific point in a single sentence. To facilitate building the diagram, it's easiest if you write each sentence on a separate index card or Post-it® Note.

As you examine what participants have said, you'll quickly see that the ideas cluster into several rather distinct general areas. For example, categories that often appear include communications, organizational structure, IT, marketing, and sales. Sort the statements into "data buckets"—groups of statements that are related to the general category under which each seems to fit. Put general statements that don't really fit into any single category in a separate location.

You can either use appropriate software for building a cause/effect diagram, or you can move the cards/labels around by hand, sticking them to a wall, white board, or large sheet of paper. Use the mission statement as your lead statement in the diagram. To its right, put a key statement that focuses on resolving issues; it might be something like, "Difficulties and deficiencies in accomplishing the mission." Put the rest of the statements to the right of your key statement. If you have identified five general categories, there will be five statements—one above the other, just to the right of the key statement. Finally, you'll break each general category into statements that relate back to the lead statement (the one farthest to the left on the diagram). In most cases, the statements will cluster naturally into cause/effect groups. Statements about more generalized concerns will generally be placed near the left side of the diagram. As issues that are descriptions of more specific concerns are added, they will be placed to the right, thereby creating a tree-like diagram that illustrates all of the concerns that participants will have identified. This process is continued until all the issues collected as data appear on the chart in a position that roughly reflects a cause/effect relationship.

Connecting all of the issues in the diagram is the word *because*. For example, if one of your main statements/categories is "The IT department needs to be strengthened," insert *because* before the next item, which may be,

"Company XYZ needs a more aggressive training program for its IT staff." Use the same technique to connect every statement in the diagram.

Let Participants Examine the Diagram

As soon as you've finished the diagram, let the group that gave you the data examine the diagram. Almost always, people will suggest changes; they may suggest that the cause/effect structure may be more accurate by moving some issues to another location. They may also suggest some additions to the data as they see what others have contributed. Make those changes immediately. Once the diagram has been edited by all the participants, it will contain every issue that they believe is critical to accomplishing the mission you've identified. In effect, the diagram can be thought of as containing all of the agenda items to be considered in the mass meeting that your company would hold if it decided to address every issue that every participant felt was important. Because such an agenda would be overwhelming, it is preferable to determine which of the many issues they have identified would be most critical in moving the organization along the preferred path.

Assign Weights

The next step is to ask the participants to determine which issues they believe are most critical. You'll need to instruct the participants to acquaint themselves with every issue on the chart, to try to understand what the frame of mind must have been for the person who suggested the issue, and to judge the relevancy of each issue from his or her own position. In order to determine the priority of the issues, each participant should mentally weigh four factors (the same four factors used in the full PriorityPath® process):

- How important is the issue?
- How familiar are you with the issue?
- How frequently does the issue occur, or could it occur?
- What relative level of effort would be required to fix or avoid the issue in the future?

Ask the participants to consider more than just how important the issue is. They are to weigh, in a very practical sense, the amount of knowledge they have about the issue; what the probable frequency of the issue may be; and the amount of time, energy, and resources that would be required to address, fix, mitigate, or avoid the impacts of each issue. Assessments of priority based only upon a single criterion are of little value unless participants also reveal their level of knowledge about the issue, their sense of its frequency, and the amount of effort it would take to address the issue.

After participants have answered all four questions about each issue in their minds, ask each one to select four (or maybe a few more) issues that he or she believes are the most critical, based on their assessment of the four factors. Give each participant four colored adhesive dots, using a different colored dot for each participating group, and ask that the dots be placed on the issues that are most critical, wherever they appear in the diagram. They may be placed on issues appearing on the left side of the diagram, indicating that the generalized comment that has numerous sub-issues to its right are areas of major concern. Some dots may be placed to the extreme right on issues that are not broken into component parts, indicating that the identified root cause issue is of major critical importance. Ask each person to use his or her own judgment in determining where to place the colored dots.

Depending on your organization, you may need to protect confidentiality. In one situation, a senior executive participated in an Abacus project along with about thirty of his intermediate and junior executives. Because of the organization's culture, the junior executives were reluctant to have anyone—especially the senior executive—know where he or she put a dot. To compensate, other people physically placed the dots on behalf of the junior executives.

Putting different colored dots for each participating group on the diagram provides an immediate and visual way of showing which issues are considered the most critical by each participating group. Participants can also see which issues individuals feel are most critical, but that the larger group does not support as critical.

In most cases, the dots placed on the diagram cluster into several well-defined areas. These represent basic "theme" areas that participants agree are of significant concern to the entire group. The dots also show where senior executives and others do and do not agree. The points of disagreement will become your focal points for securing better organizational alignment and for resolving areas of organizational conflict—and will be where you will want to pursue focused problem-solving processes.

Develop Remedial Activities

The final step is to come up with an action plan—the steps that will remedy the issues you've identified as most critical. These don't vary significantly between a full PriorityPath® project and an Abacus project; they are based on what you have learned and the priorities you have measured. You'll find a detailed description of how to set up and execute your action plan in the next chapter.

Sample Three-Day Abacus Project

Following is a sample outline of a three-day Abacus project. You should be able to easily modify this outline to meet your organization's needs. The outline is based on an actual Abacus project that was conducted by a public service organization that was trying to formulate a strategic plan. Approximately thirty people—from the CEO to a representative group of front-line staff—participated; because the agency was a public service organization, participants also included elected representatives and members of the general public. Each person was chosen carefully so all known viewpoints were represented, and each participant was known as someone who would freely express his or her views.

Day One
- **AM** Introduction
  Expectations and Objectives for the Three Days
  Explanation of The PriorityPath® and Abacus Processes
  Information-Gathering in the Large Group (Facilitator records input)
- **PM** Formation of Small Groups
  Small Group Identification of Issues and Causes (Facilitator records input)
- **EVE** Construction of Database Diagram by Facilitators

Day Two
- **AM** Validation (Editing) of Database by All Participants
  Selection of Priorities—Placement of Colored Dots on Critical Issues
- **PM** Analysis of Priorities—Selection of Major Themes
  Presentation on Preparation of Recommendations (See Chapter 11)
  Begin Formulating Recommendations in Groups

Day Three
- **AM** Complete Formulation of Recommendations
- **11:00** Presentation of Recommendations by Group Leaders
- **PM** Presentation of Recommendations (Continued)
  (*Note:* Recommendations will undergo additional research and editing before presentation to management for inclusion in strategic plan)
  Concluding Activities

CHAPTER 11

TRANSLATING FINDINGS TO ACTION: WHERE TO GO FROM HERE

An effective PriorityPath® or Abacus project isn't finished until you've done one last important thing: develop the action steps that define where your organization will go from here based on what you've learned about your priorities. All the information in the world won't be worth much unless you *use* it to remedy the issues your team has defined as critical to achieving your mission.

Major Themes

The major themes that face your organization will become evident as you go through the process of identifying issues. Those themes will result from direct findings—the things participants identify during interviews that are then grouped into categories and placed in a diagram—as well as from indirect, alignment, and implied findings.

Direct findings are those issues, reported as priorities, in rank order of importance that appear on the cause/effect diagram and in the report document.

Indirect findings include the issues that informed people know are critical, but that may not have been given that kind of recognition when the issues were rated. Indirect findings will usually come to light in formal or informal meetings you hold to talk about the meaning of project results.

Alignment findings can be seen by comparing the Strategic Event Value numbers between and among groups, noting where there is congruence and divergence about the importance of particular issues. Where there are differences in perceptions, discussion of the reasons for those differences can lead to better alignment between and among individuals and groups.

Implied findings come up as you consider how your direct findings interact with each other and with other organizational components that were not necessarily identified as issues when data was gathered. As you go over those findings, you may recognize significant overarching themes that were not specifically identified in the analysis, but that should also be considered important.

Chapter 11 • Translating Findings to Action   95

We've learned from experience that it's important to address the concerns that evolve from extracting indirect, alignment, and implied findings, and that grouping these concerns into themes, together with themes derived from examining direct findings, is often more effective than trying to deal independently with them individually, as pieces of the overall problem.

Major themes can also come up during the period *after* participants rate the importance of the issues but *before* you issue recommendations for next actions. It's important to realize that situations continually change—and it's essential that you accommodate any new conditions in the recommendations you make.

The major themes are identified and prioritized by the steering committee. To determine priorities for the critical themes, the steering committee should look at how unanimous the participating groups were about:

- How serious the theme is
- The probable impact the theme will have on accomplishing the mission
- What resources will be needed to address the theme
- The degree of urgency associated with scheduling remediation activities

Considering these criteria will help you determine how much attention you should devote to resolving the issues that comprise each theme.

Remediation Teams—Focus on System Improvement

We call the remedial activity that happens after PriorityPath® projects by the generic name of *system improvement*. You'll need to organize several teams to address the priority issues during the system improvement phase. These will be a remediation team and several theme teams. Their responsibilities will be as follows:

- The remediation team takes overall responsibility for coordinating the remedial activity—the things your organization does to resolve the issues that have been identified. The remediation team consists of a team leader, a communications coordinator, and the team leader of each theme team. (The steering committee you used during the project can be used as your remediation team.)
- A theme team needs to be assigned for each theme you've identified. Each theme team then addresses one major theme and the issues that comprise it.

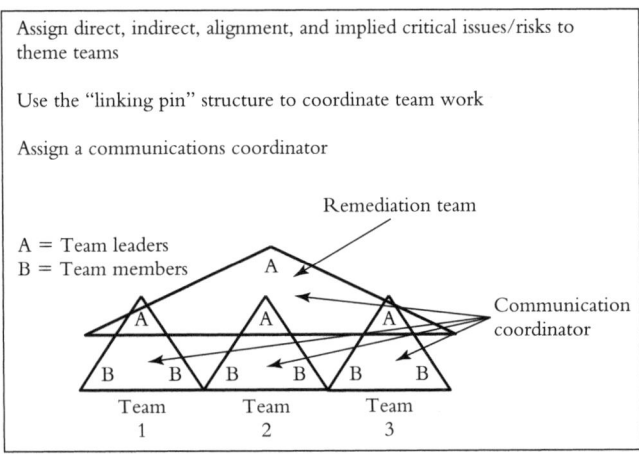

Figure 9 Initiating Theme Team Activities

Make sure that every interested employee has the opportunity to participate in examining themes, to voice opinions about issues, to explore possible solutions, and to help formulate and present recommendations. Involvement in identifying and addressing issues creates ownership of the remedial activity that will be necessary to resolve them.

The "Linking Pin": The Relationship of Remediation and Theme Teams

Teams should be linked as shown conceptually in Figure 9. The top triangle represents the remediation team, which includes the team leaders of the theme teams as well as other members who will assess the viability of recommendations made by the theme teams.

Successful Team Management

To help prepare the theme teams for their role in addressing priority themes and issues, make sure the team leaders understand the basic principles of successful team management. We've listed some literature on successful team management in the references at the end of Part 2; make sure the team leaders have access to at least some of these.

You'll find that the remedial activity we recommend during system improvement goes beyond many high-profile programs you may be familiar with—including many quality improvement programs—because it follows and is built upon accurate diagnoses of areas of critical need from both internal and external sources *before* the team is assigned to address and resolve any of the issues. As your organization begins the system improvement phase, then, your theme teams will be focused on those areas where you know your people believe improvement is needed. Their motivation to improve will be strong. The probability, therefore, is extraordinarily high that the actions they recommend will be focused, practical, and will result in the most profound positive effects possible.

As a brief summary, your team leaders should understand the following seven team management principles.

Commitment of Key Personnel

System improvement cannot be a one-person show. At a minimum, the first level of your organization's management *must* be convinced of the worth of the remediation process. High-level and middle-management people will need to display confidence in the process, faith in their subordinates, and the courage to be *leaders* rather than mere managers.

The team approach is built on the premise that intelligence in your organization is randomly distributed—that people at every level of your organization are just as likely to have intelligent ideas for system improvement as the people who are above them in the hierarchy. Senior officers in your organization need to assure you that they will respond to recommendations from remediation and theme teams with one of the following responses:

- "Approved!"
- "Before I can approve this, I need the following specific information...."
- "I can't approve the recommendation for these specific reasons...."

Team members who get these clear and reasonable responses can act quickly on approvals or can appropriately rethink and recycle. Subsequently, they can resubmit initially rejected recommendations in a form and with supplementary evidence of the wisdom of the recommendation so that it has a better chance of being approved.

Challenge your teams to be creative when recommending solutions that require funding. Team members can always suggest budget cuts in areas of lower priority to accommodate the funds for priority actions they know will improve operations.

Commitment of the Remediation Team

System improvement must be guided by a high-level remediation team that is committed to the program. This kind of work has an impact on every division and person in your organization, so it's important that every person feel that his or her views and particular needs are represented in the discussions that take place before recommendations are made. For that reason, your remediation team needs to be composed of people who are high enough in your organization to speak for their departments with authority, and that all departments are represented. The prestige of this overall leadership team helps lay the foundation for the eventual success of the process.

Focus on System Improvement

The first objective of the remediation team must be to bring the concept of system improvement into sharp focus. Team members might need to review some of the Continuous Improvement and Quality literature, so they're all working with a common vocabulary. During several long—and probably spirited—discussions, the team will come up with a set of definitions and goals to guide the remediation activity. People in your organization need to understand the relevance of their commitment to system improvement as the way they'll improve all aspects of the organization.

System improvement provides the focus for the improvement of operations in any organization—so, as a basic, the remediation team must define for itself what it means by *system improvement* and what objectives it has for transforming your organization into one that exemplifies excellence. Everything from then on focuses every person on precisely what it will take to achieve their agreed-upon goal of accomplishing the objectives they have defined.

A Unified Plan

Long experience has shown that system improvement doesn't happen unless an organization produces and follows a well-defined plan. Outside help is often useful, but until the plan is internalized and owned by the people who will be affected by it, the plan is of limited benefit. Your aim is to enlist everyone in the improvement effort and to make sure that the parts of the plan can readily be mastered by anyone. Ideally, everyone who works in your organization should eventually be assigned to work on a theme team—the entire staff will then benefit from the ideas of employees who ordinarily do not volunteer as well as from those who regularly give input.

As time progresses, the teams themselves will get a sense of how well they are doing by noting that their efforts and recommendations are being implemented to the benefit of the entire organization.

Training

All people in your organization will need training in five basic foundation activities of successful system improvement programs:

- Identify Customer Wants and Needs
- Map Processes and Procedures
- Eliminate, Simplify, and Focus
- Measure Performance
- Improve Continuously

There are other general skills that the process depends on as well, so you may need to provide some training if your organization is weak in those areas. For example, team leaders and members must be able to express their ideas clearly so others can understand the programs they suggest. They must also be proficient in exploring alternatives, writing recommendations, and knowing when to consult outside experts.

Middle and top managers will need to have good leadership skills; formal planning, organizing, implementing, and measuring will need to be done by managers, but because all employees will be participating, managers will need to manage in ways that emphasize total system improvement. For some, there may be new duties involved as managers work with groups—including counseling, providing resources, and helping them think for themselves. You'll need to help managers shift focus from measuring results to measuring performance and process, meeting customer needs, and making sure that employees identify positively with the organization. It is in these areas—not in overemphasizing bottom-line results—where improvement will translate into the results your organization wants.

Managers and team leaders should carefully consider available resources and, where the need has been carefully assessed, must have access to outside resource people. These external sources can provide training and technical expertise to make sure that all teams and employees are well prepared to resolve the issues they tackle.

Progress will almost instantly end if you allow attitudes of disrespect for employees to predominate. As one-time General Electric Chairman John R. Welch, Jr., put it, "We are going to win on our ideas—not by whips and chains."

Recognition, Gratitude, and Celebration

Every person must clearly hear "thank you" in a way that is meaningful to him or her. That thanks must happen as soon as possible, it must reflect the involvement and gratitude of top management, and it must be enjoyable. Your remediation team will need to spend some time developing the recognition programs that will be used in your organization.

Communication

System improvement goes a long way toward opening communication channels across all levels—in fact, a successful system improvement process generally opens lines of communication that may have been neglected for years. Communication between levels will not happen unless a conduit has been created.

As part of the system improvement process, you'll need to find effective ways to receive and distribute information about the process. Someone high in your organization should fill the role of communications coordinator; he or she will be the spokesperson for system improvement and will oversee day-to-day functions once the process has been launched. The coordinator will need to be convincing in contacts with teams and management personnel; be creative, persistent, flexible, and patient as information is transmitted; be trusted to make essential decisions on behalf of the groups; and must report those decisions to the groups as soon as possible.

Make sure you preserve the communication coordinator's access to top management so that there is continuous communication of decisions, issues, concerns, and recommendations in both directions.

Theme Teams

The following need to be done by each theme team:

1. Select an assistant team leader who can share responsibilities and tasks.
2. Select a team recorder/secretary that will keep minutes, write letters, write action plans, and so on. While paperwork should be kept to a minimum, one person needs to be responsible for any that is required.
3. Determine your own rules of operation—how you will run meetings, whether you will use Robert's Rules of Order, and what format you will use to submit your team's recommendations and action plans.

4. Try to achieve consensus whenever possible; when consensus isn't possible, the majority rules. Team members need to support decisions made by a majority vote—a person who disagrees should work within the team to persuade other team members, but should avoid open opposition to their decisions.
5. Accept input to your team from any and every employee in the organization.
6. As appropriate, refer some of your recommendations to other teams.
7. Keep the group focused on making relevant recommendations and implementing fixes to problems.
8. If any new issues related to your theme emerge, your team should address them as soon as they arise. Although members of teams should be changed from time to time, addressing issues in teams should be a permanent way to secure system improvement.
9. Use common sense—operate in practical ways that you know will work.

Preparing Recommendations

As a theme team, work on recommendations as follows.

1. Select an issue to work on.
   - Start by identifying key issues from the PriorityPath® diagrams and documents, whether using the full process or the Abacus version. These diagrams are "process maps" that focus attention on the priority areas where remedial action can have the greatest positive impact.
   - Examine any audit documents.
   - Identify and work on new priorities as they arise—and remember that there is nothing more permanent than change. Within a very brief time you may be faced with new but allied issues that will require concentrated attention.
   - Distinguish between *urgent* and *important* issues and between *common* and *special* causes of trouble. You'll get the best results when effort is spent on *important and special* issues, not on *urgent and common* ones. You may use appropriate statistical process control techniques, Pareto charts, or a host of other approaches in making these decisions.
2. When a solution is readily apparent, immediately recommend to management that they fix the problem. Write a letter, issue

a directive, clarify a policy or procedure, or appoint someone to take necessary action.
3. Where the solution to the problem is *not* readily apparent, try to find as many possible solutions as you can by:
   - Talking to others on the project.
   - Talking to people in the organization (or to those outside the organization as appropriate).
   - Get a specialist to help investigate possible solutions to the issue. These specialists could include university experts, specialists in training and administrative problems, lawyers, OH&S people, or organizational/product inspectors, for example.
   - Read about the issues, referring to Best Practices compilations in magazines, books, or on the Internet. People often find pieces of good solutions somewhere else that can be adapted to fit their own organization.
4. As an entire team, choose the best possible solution—the one that best meets the situation in your organization. As you make your choice, consider the following:
   - Availability of the solution: Can you get it and use it?
   - Are the skills and/or training available?
   - Are funds available? Is it worth the cost? Can you defend the cost?
   - Is the time right for this particular fix?
   - Will supervisors and managers support the idea?
5. Write a recommendation that you believe can be approved; format your paper as suggested in the following section. Then send your recommendation up the line to the remediation team. The remediation team will consider the background and implications of your recommendation and, if they approve, will send it on to management for action. The communications coordinator will help finalize the recommendation, so his or her input will be represented in the recommendation. After he or she takes your team's recommendations up the line, he or she will make sure you receive one of the three responses discussed above in a timely manner.
6. If your recommendation is returned with a request for specific additional information, get the information quickly and resubmit your recommendation.
7. If your recommendation is denied with reasons given, rework the recommendation, show how the reasons for not approving can be overcome, provide optional ways of accomplishing the intent of the

recommendation, and resubmit your recommendation. As long as you know what the objections are, you can find ways to accommodate many of them.
8. If your recommendation is approved, find out who is assigned to implement it. Implementation may be assigned to your team or it may go to another group that has specific responsibility for the area you have worked on. If your team gets the nod, draw up a plan for implementation, then carry it out. Implementation consists of:
   - Making a specific plan for carrying out the intent of the approved recommendation.
   - Assembling the necessary resources to implement the recommendations. These resources may require changes or additions to the budget, people assignments, materials, equipment, administrative structures, training, plant priorities, and schedules—whatever is needed.
   - Doing it!

How to Format Your Recommendations

- List the date, team leader, and team members.
- List the major theme area and the specific issues or problems with which the recommendation will deal. Include the background of the issue: What is the problem? On what basis can you confirm that it is a real problem? How will fixing it make a difference?
- Identify where the issue(s) came from. Was it identified as a priority in the PriorityPath® or Abacas analysis? Was it an item in an audit document? Is it a new, important, or special issue?
- List the alternative solutions to the problem that your team considered before deciding on the one you present in the recommendation.
- List the specialists, literature, Internet sites, or other sources you consulted before you decided on the solution you chose.
- Describe the solution you chose, the reasons you chose it, and the factors you considered in making the choice. For example, you might include a discussion of the availability of the solution, the skills and training that are both needed and available, the availability of funds, factors related to timing (is now the right time?), and political factors (both internal and external).
- Write the recommendation carefully, precisely, and clearly so people know exactly what you are recommending. Mention why you believe

your recommendation can or should be approved, what approving it will do for the organization, any problems it may cause, any part of the original problem that the recommendation does not deal with adequately, and any other relevant information.
- On the front page of the recommendation, list three possible responses for use of the approving officer:
  - Approved
  - Before approval, this specific information is needed. . . .
  - Not approved for these specific reasons. . . .
- After getting input from the communications coordinator, submit your recommendation to the remediation team for their consideration and submission to management.

APPENDICES

APPENDIX A

INSTRUCTIONS FOR RATING

Background

During the past several weeks, those who were invited to participate have given us information about the issues they think must be addressed to successfully achieve your organizational mission. We've incorporated the information into an analytical software tool that will show the most important issues and how much people agree on the importance of those issues. Finally, we will develop an action plan to address and resolve the issues, optimizing your capability to achieve your mission.

Rating Criteria

You will be asked to rate each item on some or all of the criteria (see Fig. 10). You may not be presented with all four judgments for each of the items because of their relationship to other items.

Rating Guidelines

- *Current status of the organization:* Rate each item according to how your organization is functioning right now—not on how it may have functioned in the past.
- *Your opinion matters:* Rate each item based on your observations and insights, not on the opinions or insights of others.
- *Blank ratings:* Leave boxes blank if:
  - You can't offer an informed judgment (the issue is not within your realm of expertise or it deals with something that does not affect you).
  - The issues express ideas that you know are not true.
  - The issues express ideas with which you disagree.

Relationship among Issues

- Consider each group of issues independently from any other group of issues you have seen.
- Each group of issues is preceded by a "leading" issue that is followed by the statement, "Because . . . " Rate each issue that follows as it relates to the "leading" issue that precedes it.

Importance	How much does this issue currently affect you and/or is it likely to affect you in the future if it is not appropriately addressed and resolved?	0: the issue does not need to be addressed 1: not important 2: minimally important 3: moderately important 4: important 5: highly important
Familiarity	How familiar are you with the issue?	Low: unfamiliar with the issue Medium: somewhat familiar with issue High: very familiar with the issue
Frequency	How often does the issue occur OR how often could it occur?	Low: seldom Medium: periodically High: regularly
Remediation	What would be the level of effort to eliminate or moderate the issue?	Low: minimal effort Medium: moderate effort High: extensive effort

Figure 10 Critical Event Rating Criteria

- Recognize that each sub-issue has a slightly different point that needs to be assessed separately from other issues.

Timing

- The rating instrument will be available on the Internet from (*date*) to (*date*).
- Plan to devote approximately one hour for rating for each 150 items in the database.
- If at any time during the rating process you want to step away, you may log off and come back later to continue and complete the process. Make sure you complete the process within the designated time period and that you use the same user name and password.

If you have suggestions for additions or changes to this database, please send them to us via e-mail. We will report the suggestions we receive together with the priorities of all participants as soon as possible.

The e-mail address for responses is info@prioritysystems.net.

Thank you for your participation.

You are now ready to begin the rating process.

Organizations that want to use Rating Booklets instead of the Internet will have similar instructions printed in the booklets.

APPENDIX B

WHAT CLIENTS HAVE TO SAY

"Where PriorityPath® goes beyond the other methodologies is in the discipline of the process, the gathering and processing (quantification) of risks, the efficient and effective involvement of the customers in the process, and the ability to perform additional analysis at lower cost the second, third, and 'N' number of times once a database is developed." *John Kingsley, Kingsley Associates, Washington, D.C.*

"The final product was so well documented that there was absolutely no argument from any party about the findings." *Dr. J.D. Harder, Board Member, Canadian Food Grains Bank*

"I would not hesitate to use your firm again and would recommend you without reservation to other companies wanting to improve their operation, productivity, profitability, or quality." *David Mayfield, Executive Vice President and General Manager, Philips BTS*

"The in-depth information gathering, the knowledge used to create a cooperative, meaningful liaison between factions, complemented by a comprehensive final report, verified our confidence in the selection of this firm. I would strongly endorse the use of this procedure to business and community groups alike." *Former Alderman Les Pears, City of Calgary*

"I would personally recommend your organization and your analysis techniques to anyone who is attempting to establish a program to resolve any complex set of issues similar to those with which we were challenged with at Twin Butte." *G.W. Stephens, Manager, Foothills Operations for Shell Canada*

"I believe this procedure to be a valuable tool in assessing the corporate milieu in that it provides an ability to differentiate and define the relationship between organization symptoms, and more generic causal issues." *David H. Rehill, Executive Director, Recreation and Parks*

"I would suggest that if the Defendant could show that he had taken all reasonable steps to reduce or eliminate hazards (through use of PriorityPath® procedures) that Courts would be much less likely to impose punitive damages, and the potential exists in those circumstances that the quantum of regular damages could be reduced as well." *John A. Thompson, Barrister*

"Priority Systems® . . . reliably performs the work they are contracted to do. Comparing profiles of priority among key individuals and major groups permits creative strategy development that is unique. Results translate into action rapidly due to the deep involvement of all of the individuals and groups that are affected by the area under examination. My decision to use them again . . . is based on my experience that their analytical system produces actionable results in ways that I have not experienced with any other analytical approach." *Gary Holden, Former Chairman and CEO, EnSource Industries; President AltaGas*

"Vista was an ambitious and relatively undefined project. It involved months of research and involvement with providers and users of student services. However, through the excellent work of Priority Systems®, the Vista team was able to both boil the ocean and to distill the essential and relevant issues associated with the delivery of student services. Our sincerest appreciation goes to Priority Systems® for their quality work and going beyond the mark." *Gary L. Kramer, Associate Dean, Admissions and Records, Brigham Young University*

"Your ability to identify the high priority issues our company faces from the hundreds of issues raised by our employees was fascinating. We were able to reduce a large number of issues through memos and meetings. Significant improvement has been made on the highest priority issues through employee meetings, internal communications, and by forming teams to work on specific issues. Our goal of being viewed by our employees as a single global company has been improved significantly." *Jeff Bloomer, CEO, IFR Inc., Wichita, KS*

"Priority Systems® was contracted to evaluate critical success factors in the planning process and facilitate, via their PriorityPath® system, an analysis and identification of possible concerns with respect to those same success factors. Priority Systems® helped focus cooperative efforts towards the resolution of several critical problem areas. Their efforts in assisting the planning team to identify and rank order priorities, highly relevant and important to the success of the overall Summit, was of great utility. There is no question Priority Systems® aided the Summit Security Planning Team that ultimately led to one of the most peaceful Summits ever held." *Rick Hanson, Deputy Chief, Bureau of Community Policing*

Appendix C

Partial Client List

Federal Government

United States
  Army (multiple projects)
  Navy (multiple projects)
  Department of Defense (numerous classified and unclassified projects)
  Department of Agriculture
  Department of the Interior (multiple projects)
  Executive Office of the President
  Veterans Administration

Canada
  Coast Guard
  Department of Indian and Northern Affairs
  Department of Transport
  RCMP/Calgary Police Services

New Zealand
  Army
  Department of Defense
  Wholesale Electricity Marketing Development Group

State and Provincial Governments

Alberta
  Alberta Cabinet, Deputy Ministers and MLAs
  Alberta Workers' Compensation Board
  Department of Advanced Education
  Department of Culture
  Department of Education
  Department of Environment
  Department of Manpower
  Department of Natural Resources
  Department of Recreation and Parks
  Department of Social Services
  Department of Occupational Health and Safety

California
Department of Education (multiple projects)

Hong Kong Government
Drainage Services Department

Ontario
Department of Justice

Tasmania and New South Wales, Australia
Hunter Water Board
Sydney Water Board
Tasmania Hydro

Utah
Department of Community and Economic Development
Department of Social Services
Division of Water Resources
State Tax Commission

Local Government

Alberta
City of Edmonton

New Zealand
City of Hastings
City of Tauranga
Gisborne District Council

Ohio
Cuyahoga Metropolitan Housing Authority, Cleveland
Greater Cincinnati Water Works, Cincinnati

Oregon
United Sewage Agency
Washington County Economic Development

Schools and School Systems

Alberta
City of Calgary
Counties of Newell, Warner, and Vulcan
Counties of Parkland, Camrose, and Mountain View
Ten School Authorities in the Bonnyville/Cold Lake Region

United States
  Brigham Young University, Provo, Utah
  University of California, Hayward and San Luis Obispo
  Hundreds of Schools in California, Maryland, New York, Illinois,
    Florida, Ohio, Utah, and Washington, D.C.

Health Care

  Bright Medical Clinic, Whittier, CA
  Intermountain Health Care (four facilities in Utah)
  Kaiser-Permanente, San Jose, CA
  Mayo Clinic, Phoenix, AZ
  Multi Care Health System, Tacoma, WA
  Saint Patrick Hospital, Missoula, MT
  Stevens Memorial Hospital, Edmonds, WA
  Sullivan/Luallin, San Diego, CA (multiple projects)
  Sutter Health System (three facilities in California)
  Virginia Mason Consortium Hospitals (three facilities)
  Virginia Mason Hospital and Clinic, Seattle, WA

Commercial Clients

  AGT Limited
  American Airlines
  Armco Steel
  AT&T
  Amoco
  Bechtel
  Boeing
  Boeing Computer Services
  Bonneville Corporation
  British Petroleum (BP)
  Calgary Winter Olympics
  California Edison
  Chem-Security (Alberta) Limited
  CitiBank
  Cooper Petroleum Company
  DuPont
  EnSource Energy Services Inc.
  Esso Resources
  General Telephone

Genstar
Guarantee Savings and Loan (23 branches)
Hercules
Hyundai Heavy Industries
I.F.R. Systems
Information Systems (Worldwide Network Assessment)
J.R. Simplot Minerals and Chemical Group
Royal KLM (Dutch Airline)
Knoxville Volunteer Rescue Squad, Knoxville, TN
KPMG (Peat Marwick, multiple projects)
Laidlaw Waste Management
Marconi Test Instruments
McDonnell Douglas
Montgomery Ward
Montgomery Watson Harza (environmental projects)
Morton Thiokol
New Zealand Telecom
Northwest Development Corp.
Nova Gas Ltd.
Petro-Canada
Philips Broadcast Television Systems
Philips Consumer Electronics Corporation (multiple projects)
Plessey Electronic Systems Ltd., England and Australia
Portland General Electric
Precision Castparts
Presbyterian Church, Falls Church, VA
Procter & Gamble
Rocky Mountain Helicopters
Security Pacific Bank
Sikorsky Helicopters
Suncor (two projects)
Syncrude Canada Ltd. (eight projects)
Taylor Preston Meat Packing, Wellington, NZ
Vaughn Manufacturing
Westinghouse (five divisions)
Wickes Companies
World Food Grains Bank

We will be pleased to discuss particular applications of the approaches we used.

Appendix D

Project Summaries: Resolving Controversial and Complex Issues, Achieving Measurable Results

Priority Systems® has been successful in helping clients address a wide variety of issues; the project summaries included in this Appendix illustrate the range of applications that have successfully used our technology. It's important to note that we have often facilitated communication between antagonistic or noncommunicative groups, usually over areas that have been controversial or complex in nature. More often than not, we've been able to help these clients achieve results that they could measure.

Because many of the specific findings of these projects are confidential, we're restricted in the amount of detail we can provide about each one. Nevertheless, we have tried to describe things well enough that you can see the variety of issues we've worked on—and the many benefits that can be derived from PriorityPath® projects.

We hope that as you examine these project descriptions you'll be able to see how you could resolve issues and enjoy success by identifying your organization's missing components and analyzing the factors that inhibit progress. Reading these descriptions might also motivate you to more rigorously consider alternate approaches in your efforts to improve situations in your organization. Remember, you can accomplish more by just asking yourself "What more should we add to make this work better?" and "What factors do we need to recognize and control to prevent things from going wrong?"

We hope, too, that you will be more cognizant of your organization's limitations and that you will try to address issues in ways that are presented in this book. Whether your work occurs incidentally, you use the Abacus system, or you use the more rigorous approaches of the full PriorityPath® process, you'll realize considerable benefits when you determine priorities based on these three questions: What is missing? What generic problems do we need to solve? What do we need to do today to prevent the problems that seem to be approaching?

A. Commercial Clients

A Commercial Airline

A large U.S. airline company used the PriorityPath® process to address issues it was experiencing with lost baggage and ground damage to aircraft. When our project began, the airline was rated eighth on the U.S. Department of Transportation rating scale for effectiveness and efficiency in handling passenger baggage. The airline was also experiencing significant losses through damage to aircraft while on the ground. Contact with other aircraft, collisions with vehicles, and breakage of aircraft parts during loading and unloading were all too common.

We interviewed ground and flight crews, supervisors, and managers at company headquarters and at seventeen of the airline's hubs located in the United States and internationally. We collected responses about what could be done better, what existing problems needed more attention, and anticipated future problems. We formatted all of these into the PriorityPath® logic diagram, which was edited and validated at each site by those who had contributed and then rated the information for relative significance.

The results were reported for each area of concern. In one set of report documents, the priorities for improving baggage handling were evident. In the other set of reports, the priorities for limiting damage to aircraft on the ground were revealed.

The company immediately set priorities for changes that would improve the airline's performance in both handling baggage and preventing aircraft damage on the ground. Some of these changes originated from headquarters, but many more were formulated in each of the seventeen hub airports, where input from those who had participated in assessing conditions could be continued.

Some innovative solutions were adopted. For instance, at one airport the senior management team altered the content of the Daily Dependability Meeting agenda that it had long followed. Instead of having managers simply review emergent matters and deal with routine concerns, the meetings were structured to focus on the same types of issues that had been examined in the PriorityPath® program. A system of rotation among meeting attendees was implemented so that every employee had an opportunity to attend a Daily Dependability Meeting about once every six weeks.

Each meeting started with an analysis of what had gone wrong in the previous twenty-four hours; attendees then examined worries about existing conditions or future eventualities. Each person was also asked to contribute his or her judgments about new things that needed to be done. The balance of the meeting was devoted to generating specific plans to make sure that none of the concerns mentioned in the meeting would happen on that day. Participants also talked about upcoming activities—such as the need for major inter-line baggage transfers when a charter flight either arrived or left the station—and how they planned to handle problems occasioned by changes in the weather.

While the PriorityPath® analysis certainly delivered a short list of actions that needed to be taken immediately, the station manager said it also provided significant value by helping managers focus more precisely on avoiding the hazards, weaknesses, and problems that had too often simply been ignored. By modifying the content of the Daily Dependability Meetings, he was able to perpetuate the process benefits that had been learned during the PriorityPath® project. The issues were clearly anticipated and examined each morning—so instead of spending each day in his office dealing with emergent problems, the station manager was able to walk around the airport, providing encouragement to his staff and becoming more familiar with all parts of the operation.

During the next eighteen months, the airport's financial reports showed that tens of millions of dollars were saved by improved baggage handling and by limited damage to aircraft on the ground. During this eighteen-month period, the airline's U.S. Department of Transportation rating for careful handling of baggage improved from number eight to number one among America's commercial airlines.

Water Management Projects

A large international engineering firm that specializes in supply of culinary water and treatment of waste water has used Priority Systems® on numerous occasions to address a number of critical issues.

Revenue Enhancement

One project dealt with the need of a Midwestern city to expand its revenue-producing activities. The city's exemplary water system is recognized for its excellent quality throughout the nation. Unfortunately, it was built to supply a projected population greater than that which currently resides in the municipality. Furthermore, many residents have moved to neighboring bedroom communities where utilities are provided by other municipal organizations. Two simultaneous problems have resulted: (1) Revenues in the major center are falling, but the cost of maintaining the system—which was built to serve a larger population—is not declining. (2) In the bedroom communities, the shifting population is demanding more services.

The city hired an engineering firm to help them find ways to maintain the current system and offer services to communities in the surrounding area. The engineering firm asked that Priority Systems® help the city explore alternatives.

We met with approximately forty city and engineering firm managers and staff to explore areas that should be pursued, problems that needed to be overcome, and potential issues. The resulting information was placed in the typical database, edited, and rated for relevance by the participants.

The results were used as the basis for the engineering firm's report about practical alternatives that should be pursued. It included recommendations for partnering with the outlying communities.

System Rehabilitation

Another project with the same firm involved helping a very old, very large water system rehabilitate its culinary water supply. Participants in the analysis were drawn from engineers who were experienced in the actual system as well as senior and experienced engineers who would be involved in the project. Priorities were prepared from the differing perspectives of that entire group of engineers, engineers who had previously been employed with the target water system, engineers who had consulted with the water system, and consultants who had not been involved with the system.

The priorities of the four groups were used to focus the presentation for executives of the water system and to outline the ways the engineering firm would fulfill the objectives of the potential client.

System Expansion

A third project with this engineering firm focused on assessing the judgments of the individuals within and working with the Utilities Department of a large western city that needed to increase its culinary water supply. The city is a bedroom community of a large metropolitan area that is experiencing rapid residential and industrial growth. Recent drought conditions in the area had heightened the interest of the community, creating conditions that favored moving forward with a major expansion project.

Interviews were held with key individuals from the engineering firm, the city council, senior city managers, the city utilities department staff, and specialist consultants working with the engineering firm and the utilities department. They identified a broad array of issues they believed would be of interest to residents and businesses in the city. These included issues relating to alignment of key participants toward the goals, objectives, and plans prepared by the project team. Administrative issues related to stakeholder support—ensuring affordability, sensitivity to costs of development engineering, securing required permits, and selection of a preferred plan—were examined in detail. Attention was also given to the need for clear communications to the public at every stage of the development program and addressing the impacts of actions taken in the project on other groups.

The prioritized results proved useful in fine-tuning the ongoing planning work.

A Chemical and Fertilizer Company

The new vice president of the Chemical and Fertilizer Division of a major agricultural products manufacturer wanted to assess the strengths of the existing operation so he could use them as a benchmark against which future progress could be measured. His responsibilities included overseeing the operation of three fertilizer installations, a large phosphates mine, and sales organizations in the western United States and throughout Canada.

Since his organization was involved in a highly competitive industry, there was significant interest in reducing production costs, optimizing every aspect of the operation, and securing early completion of one production facility that was being rebuilt. Costs of rebuilding had exceeded expectations by tens of millions of dollars in the few months before the vice president had been appointed.

The analysis focused on ensuring that the mine and the three manufacturing operations operate successfully and ensuring that management and division objectives were accomplished.

The mission statement prepared to focus the project was as follows:

To improve the profitability and productivity of the mine and manufacturing operations in the United States and Canada while creating a more synergetic workforce at headquarters and at each of the four company locations.

The following objectives were listed for the project:

- To identify, diagnose, and prioritize critical risk and alignment factors associated with achieving maximum profitability and productivity in the mine and three manufacturing operations

- To optimize use of resources
- To remove or attenuate factors that are keeping the mine and manufacturing operations from reaching full profitability and productivity potential
- To help employees working in the mine and manufacturing operations exhibit greater synergy and cooperation in addressing critical issues, thereby improving both effectiveness and efficiency

Approximately 200 people employed by the company in Idaho, Wyoming, California, and Canada answered our three basic questions—identifying what they believed was missing, what needed greater attention, and what kept them awake at night. Their responses were summarized in crisp statements and organized into a cause/effect database/diagram. Participants then edited their input to ensure that the information as presented could be understood, that the logic of the diagram was reasonable, and that no critical issues were missing.

The data was rated for relative significance. We prepared profiles of priority for managers and workers at each site, for the participants as a whole, and for the overall leadership of the company.

The priority viewpoints were used to refocus the strategic plans of the company. Some significant issues of grave importance to workers were addressed, and full attention was given to getting the third manufacturing facility back online—which was accomplished in the next few months. Production increased to more than 100 percent of rated capacity, making the entire operation much more profitable than it had been for several years.

A Canadian Power Generation Company

A major electric power generation and distribution company in western Canada was preparing to move from being regulated to being deregulated. There was considerable debate about which changes would need to be made to ensure that the company remained competitive once its monopoly status was eliminated. This focus was encapsulated in a mission statement prepared for our project with the company:

> *To ensure that the Generation Division has in place the accountabilities to be successful, particularly with respect to growth, evolving industry conditions, operations, and maintenance strategies.*

Representatives of staff at all levels in the company were asked the three typical questions used to gather data in a PriorityPath® analysis. We assembled responses into a database diagram in a cause/effect format, and participants edited the data and rated it for significance.

Interest centered primarily on management issues, the way the company would respond to the deregulated environment, anticipated risks associated with operations and maintenance, and a variety of human resource management and communications issues.

When the priorities of the participating groups were available, management structured groups to react to them and to recommend possible solutions to the major issues. When the company was actually faced with deregulation a few months later, it was prepared to adjust its practices and has continued to be successful despite major changes that have occurred in the industry.

Planning a Hazardous Waste Facility and Rubber Reclamation Plant

A major international waste handling company found an opportunity to submit a bid to build and operate a large hazardous waste facility near a major U.S. industrial city. The bidding company partnered with several people who produced, handled, and regulated industrial waste in the community, and together they decided to use the PriorityPath® process to help them prepare the bid documents.

Our analysts interviewed key people in the community, including local politicians, corporations that produce waste, and an organization that wanted to form a partnership with the bidder to operate the plant. The resulting analysis showed that the economics of the proposed installation were favorable, but there would be major challenges in addressing all of the anticipated barriers.

The bidding company continued to pursue the project, paying particular attention to the issues they now knew they would have to address. As the bid-closing date approached, it became apparent that political outmaneuverings would favor a competitor. The company used this knowledge in making the strategic decision to cancel its submission, saving the $40 million it would have wasted trying to pursue a project that evidence suggested they could never win.

The same company then found an opportunity to build and operate a rubber-grinding, tire reclamation project in the southwestern area of the United States. The company recognized the environmental headache created by dumping bulky, nonbiodegradable tires—which can't be compacted—in landfills. When tires are dumped in landfills, the sites are rapidly filled and remain an eyesore for generations.

The company found a technology for reclaiming old tires that strips out the steel inserts and recovers the fibers that give the tires the stability they need to function properly. The economics of the proposed plant seemed good as long as markets for the reclaimed tires could be found in reasonable proximity.

The company intended to focus marketing activities primarily in the state where the facility was to be located and in an adjacent state to the west. We were employed to examine priorities for selecting potential clients, both in the targeted market states and in other nearby states.

Our analysis determined that interest in purchasing the reclaimed rubber, fiber, and steel was much higher in states that had not initially been targeted for the marketing effort; as a result, the company revised its marketing plan to focus on those other states. They built the plant, successfully operated it, and assured its viability by servicing the needs of customers in the other states we identified.

Hazardous Waste Plant Expansion

A large integrated hazardous waste processing facility located in northern Canada accepted liquid and solid wastes and provided stabilization, incineration, storage, and final disposition in a secured landfill. The facility needed to be expanded because it was being pressured to accept hazardous wastes from a much larger area than had been originally planned. Along with the pressure to accommodate potential customers in a larger area, the facility needed to improve its operating efficiency and reliability.

The facility hired us to perform an operational assessment of priorities for managing the existing plant and to provide guidance for building and operating the new addition. Our mandate included helping project managers use the Priority Systems® approach as a project management tool to guide construction of the $60 million expansion. A steering committee comprised of company representatives, plant executives, and project managers formulated the following mission statement as a guide to the PriorityPath® project:

> To ensure sustained, smooth operation at or above design through-put of the proposed expansion of the plant in a safe and responsible manner through recognition of the priorities of involved individuals and groups in the construction, commissioning, startup, and operation of the expanded system.

The analysis examined the functions of people who worked in the plant, in marketing, in transportation of wastes to the plant, and the relationships of each group with the owners. Concerns and recommendations were gathered in individual interviews and then formatted into the cause/effect patterns of a typical analysis. The material was edited by project participants and rated for significance.

The priorities of the participant groups became focal points for project managers during construction of the addition. More important, however, was the analysis of administrative and management issues that were causing many of the problems in operating the plant. Marketing and transportation concerns were addressed so that the flow of materials to the plant became more regular. The addition was constructed and commissioned, management concerns were resolved, and the plant continues to operate successfully with the expanded capacity that was needed.

Information and Communication Services

A large organization that functions in most countries around the world operates a satellite-based IT network that communicates with hundreds of sites, delivering and receiving electronic data, television, and radio signals. Continuous service is essential to the operations of the organization. While the system has been in existence for several years, a desire was expressed to take action to secure 99.999 percent availability and reliability. While the goal was ambitious, people were convinced that with minor adjustments, the goal was probably attainable.

Priority Systems® was involved in providing assistance to the U.S. staff responsible for making the improvements. We interviewed all of the managers and approximately half of the people responsible for the system in the United States, and asked what needed to be done to accomplish the 99.999 percent availability goal for their communications system.

Recent changes in organizational structure had an impact on the analysis. A new senior director had been appointed to lead within a new management structure—a person whom had been recommended by his predecessor. Consequently, no one in the organization had previous experience with the new structure; it was new to everyone. The span of control had been broadened considerably, a major change from the previous structure where personnel reported to a leader whose background was similar to their own. For example, some of the managers whose skills and responsibilities were highly technical were now being managed by senior officers who did not have a technical background. These conditions had produced organizational strains.

The project identified the priorities of people at every level in the organization. Actions were taken to relieve strains, the most notable being that although the organizational structure was very new, it was rather quickly revised. The span of control for the senior executive officer was reduced to five, which greatly streamlined the structure and made it more manageable.

A Telecommunications Company

In another IT project, Priority Systems® was asked to help a telecommunications company in the southern hemisphere refine its wireless telephone services to customers throughout the country. The company had evolved from being a government-owned and controlled utility to a government-owned but independent profit-producing corporation.

The transition from being a utility to becoming a player in a new, highly competitive field presented challenges. Instead of being the monopoly provider of wireless telephone services, it faced competitors that had entered the market. One was a large European company with extensive wireless service experience and an advanced marketing and advertising program that had secured a large portion of the market within a short period of time. The local telecommunications company felt threatened by the competition, especially when its owner—namely, the government—began to require accountability from its new service entity.

Priority Systems® was engaged to help the company analyze and accomplish the following goal:

> *To identify the major risks to the achievement of the mobile telephone company's strategy, which is to grow the mobile business and to recommend ways to minimize the identified risks.*

Following the analysis, the company formulated a revised strategic plan. The new plan incorporated means that the company later used to resolve the priority issues that had been isolated in the PriorityPath® analysis.

A Major, Worldwide Consulting Practice

One of the largest consulting companies in the world has used the PriorityPath® approach on several occasions to focus company efforts on resolving critical issues in its own organization. These included focusing and aligning approaches by their state and local government practice in the United States, focusing their international practice on realistic and achievable goals for the current century, and focusing expansion of outsourcing initiatives from their eastern seaboard location.

The interest of the company centered in the capacity of PriorityPath® to generate profiles from multiple points of view. For instance, they were very interested to discover reasons for the differences in success of engagements in various locations throughout the country. They wondered why certain approaches were more successful on the East Coast than they were in the western United States—and why there were additional differences when similar approaches were used with clients in the Midwest. The company wanted to know the salient and critical factors it would face if their limited outsourcing programs were expanded.

The PriorityPath® projects included representatives of all of the groups that were involved in the areas under consideration. Data was gathered in individual interviews, in large and small group meetings, and in written submissions via e-mail. Each person interviewed provided insights into what the organization should be doing, what recurrent problems needed concentrated attention, and what fears they had about the future. This information was assembled into the usual cause/effect diagram and edited by those who had contributed the information. The same contributors of information then rated each issue for relative significance. Results were delivered to company executives, who made decisions about implementing remedial strategies to address the high-priority issues.

We were pleased when this world-renowned organization recognized that Priority Systems® assessed and delivered statements of priority on which they were able to build corporate plans for their company's progress. It was evident that the PriorityPath® approach offers unique benefits that may not yet be available to even large organizations.

Calgary Olympic Games

Approximately two and a half years before the Calgary Olympics started, the organizing committee listed the expectations of users and providers of the Results Compilation and Distribution System that would be used to report results of each event to the contestants and to the world. Involved in these discussions were people from Swiss Timing, IBM, other computer hardware and software suppliers, Alberta Government Telephones, CTV Television Network, ABC Sports, the International Olympic Committee, the Calgary Olympic Committee, the national and international sports federations, announcers, and volunteers. It soon became apparent that each group had its own agenda and was competent in its own area of responsibility.

The organizers also realized that interaction and communication among the groups needed to be improved—and that failure to make these improvements would be crucial to the overall financial success of the Olympics. The

Calgary Olympic Committee and ABC Sports had a $309 million agreement that depended on results being provided to ABC sports announcers within two to five seconds of an athlete being declared a winner. If the information was not provided within the specified time, financial penalties were to be exacted. If the system failed to meet the time deadlines for the full sixteen days of the games, revenues to the organizers would be significantly reduced.

The Olympic Committee needed to make sure that all the interested groups had effective intercommunication, so a PriorityPath® project was conducted. We asked all participants to identify needs that had not yet been addressed and to pinpoint real and potential problem areas that needed to be resolved. The results allowed participants to gain a complete understanding of how all their functions interrelated. The resulting coordination was so effective that the November 1987 trial events gave the committee confidence that it would remain in control throughout the 1988 Games. In fact, there were no problems with the Results Compilation and Distribution System during the sixteen days of the Calgary Olympic Games, and the Olympic Committee received full payment from ABC Sports and eventually realized profits of more than $250 million.

Just four months before the Games started, officials realized they needed to reexamine the ticketing function. A PriorityPath® project was initiated with members of the Ticketing Department and senior officials of the Organizing Committee. We discovered several potentially dangerous conditions through our process, and the committee decided to restructure and streamline the ticketing function. As a result, staff that had considered leaving was retained, planned programs were modified, and the Ticketing Department realized profits of several million dollars more than had been expected from ticket sales.

Projects in Medical Services

The PriorityPath® process has been used in medical services in a variety of ways.

Expansion of a Medical Clinic

We helped a large, internationally recognized specialty medical clinic expand its services from its home location in a northern state to a metropolitan area in the southwest. There were a number of logistical problems about which various opinions were expressed. The project helped focus the activity and assist in accomplishing a smooth startup for the new facility.

Nursing Shortage

We helped a large hospital organization address the nursing shortage they were facing. More than a dozen hospitals, primarily in the northwest, were having difficulty attracting and retaining nursing staff. We worked with hospital executives and staff and representatives of the nursing association to revise programs in ways that helped stem the flow of nurses from employment with their organization.

Standard Procedures

In another project, we helped a large, university-based medical research organization examine standard procedures for performing sensitive brain surgery. The procedures essential to performing the specialized surgery successfully were placed in the cause/effect format of a PriorityPath® project. Surgeons who were familiar with the procedure were then able to provide a documented flowchart of processes that must be followed. The chart allowed them to see the probable ramifications if anything began to go wrong.

Amalgamation of Medical Practices

In conjunction with a well-known medical consulting practice, we helped several large clinics streamline their organizational structures and operational procedures. When it became apparent that meeting insurance requirements was much more practical when doctors worked together in larger clinics, many who had been working alone banded together so they could better meet the new insurance requirements. This change, however, presented new challenges. Instead of each doctor being able to make decisions independently as he or she had been able to do when working alone, it became necessary that the work of each doctor be coordinated with his or her associates. We helped several of these new clinics identify and overcome the strains that appeared under the new arrangements.

Tasmania to Australia Power Transmission

A recent news item on the Basslink website states the following:

After two and half years of the most rigorous environmental and social impact assessment processes, Basslink is now in the construction phase.

The land survey is completed, Pirelli is producing the hundreds of kilometers of cable, and Siemens is preparing for construction. And in 2005 Basslink will be completed.

Basslink will create jobs and, once operational, will cement Tasmania's reputation as a source of clean, green renewable energy.

Basslink is the name given to the large engineering project initiated by Hydro Tasmania that will enable distribution of hydroelectric power generated in Tasmania to the southern Australian states. While the Australian mainland has very little ability to generate electric power in hydro stations—and very few rivers that can be dammed—Tasmania has an abundance of hydroelectric power.

Australian interest in environmental protection—in particular, their interest in the environmentally friendly "green" power produced without the need to burn hydrocarbons—provided an attractive setting for individuals and corporations that wanted to explore the exporting of power from Tasmania to the state of Victoria. The news item on the website, quoted above, indicates that the dream was scheduled to become a reality in 2005. More recently Basslink announced that commissioning is scheduled to occur in April 2006.

In late 2001, Priority Systems® was engaged by Hydro Tasmania to help the Basslink team explore issues that would need to be addressed and resolved before planning could continue. A steering committee involving Hydro Tasmania and Basslink executives, government officials in both Tasmania and Victoria, potential users of the power, environmental interests, and some members of the general public was asked to provide judgments about critical factors that needed to be considered before power could be exported to Australia.

Participants identified issues in the categories of policy, planning, organizational structure, management, asset management, operations, human resources, information technology, modeling, interactions with external organizations, and achieving a balance among engineering, financial, and commercial interests. The priorities of each of the participating groups were ascertained using the PriorityPath® process. The results, combined with those of other environmental and social impact assessments referenced in the news item, were used to focus ongoing planning activities. After considerable consultation, the planning activity continued, contracts were signed, and construction began. The addition of green power to the southern Australian grid scheduled to occur in 2006 will fulfill popular ambitions of Australian residents.

A Gas Gathering and Processing Installation in North Africa

A large U.S. construction company contracted to design and build a major natural gas gathering and processing facility in the deserts of North Africa. The design work had to accommodate the severe conditions found in the desert—meaning that the facility had to be robust enough to operate in the heat, cold, and wind of the desert. While the technological planning could easily be done by the engineering staff of the U.S. construction company, accommodating the unique requirements of the North African–based company and its access to markets presented challenges.

Our PriorityPath® analysis was tasked with ensuring that both U.S. and North African project planners would have their legitimate interests and concerns accommodated during planning. Our initial analysis was conducted with U.S. engineers and managers; later, a contingent from North Africa joined the planning group and introduced the team to the special circumstances that would be encountered in the project. For example, they explained that the team would need to stop construction for about three hours each day while the daily winds were blowing—visibility would be restricted so much that routine work could not be done. They also indicated that the plan to paint the facilities would be unnecessary—the daily winds would effectively remove paint almost immediately. They also discussed the problems that would arise from construction and operation of pipelines across the shifting sands of the Sahara Desert, the operational barriers that would be encountered, and the need for extensive training of the people that would operate the system.

Program planning proceeded until the contractor and the North African client were both confident that construction in the desert could begin at an early date. At this point, a political situation caused plans to be placed on hold for several years.

A Capital Investment Project

A group of entrepreneurs acquired exclusive interest in an Internet-based program to extend health benefits to people via the web. The group found interest among a core group of experienced people who wanted to pursue the new enterprise. They discussed a variety of ways of organizing a company to deliver the new products, and ultimately chose to use the multi-level marketing (MLM) approach, as several of the company executives had extensive experience with the MLM form of delivery of services in other health-related organizations.

They were successful in raising the initial seed money to develop their concepts, but as the marketing and development plan came together, it became apparent that more capital would be needed to launch the company.

The group approached a venture capital organization that showed significant interest, but suggested that they needed a more comprehensive presentation of the concept before it could be funded. One of the venture capital principals knew about the PriorityPath® approach and suggested that the group consider using it to demonstrate the viability of their development and marketing plans.

Accordingly, the new MLM contacted Priority Systems® for help in preparing the proposal they would use to attract an investor for their new venture. With our help, they approached several investors, and eventually found a direction that would make the new venture operational.

B. MILITARY AND SPACE PROJECTS

Deep Battle Plans

In the mid-eighties, when the Cold War was still a major worry, the U.S. Army was concerned about an offensive attack from the forces of Warsaw Pact nations. The most likely location for such an attack was near the German city of Fulda. It was here that NATO and Warsaw Pact forces faced each other in the largest peacetime concentration of military personnel and equipment in history.

From Fulda there is a broad natural corridor leading to Western Germany. This famous corridor is referred to by the military as the "Fulda Gap," and it formed the shortest pathway for the Warsaw troops to Frankfurt. Its defense was of great strategic importance to NATO.

Military planners were concerned about the overwhelming numerical superiority of Warsaw Pact troops, and better intelligence and technology would be needed to prevail should a conflict begin. PriorityPath® was used to bring focus and consensus among military leaders regarding a concept known as "Deep Battle."

Deep Battle involves the use of military assets some distance behind the frontline battle area. During the course of the PriorityPath® analysis, it became evident that military leaders and commanding officers differed in their views of what the features of the Deep Battle concept should be. If not resolved, these differences in a firefight could lead to chaos and confusion. It was imperative that consensus be established and the concept of Deep Battle be defined.

The analysis involved gathering conceptual judgments about the components of an ideal Deep Battle plan from a broad spectrum of military leaders. Once all participants were satisfied that the database was exhaustive and complete, the information they provided was placed in a cause/effect diagram and rated for significance, and the high-priority issues were highlighted.

The highlighted data showed many areas of consensus and provided the foundation for resolution of differences. This ultimately led to the development of a unified Deep Battle Army doctrine. Because of the sensitive nature of this project, specific details cannot be disclosed or discussed; however, one of the key advantages of using the PriorityPath® process was realized. The process enables stakeholders to increase their sensitivity, understanding, and acknowledgment of ideas and concepts held by other important stakeholders. We have found that a broad approach to gathering intelligence has proven vastly superior to the utilization of ideas and concepts held by single individuals. The whole is greater than the sum of its parts. It also utilizes the background and experience of major players to the betterment of the organization. In the case of Deep Battle, the group of stakeholders participating in the analysis included the majority of the Army's senior leadership, including General H. Norman Schwarzkopf, who led the first U.S. incursion into Iraq.

It has been suggested by some military personnel that the number of men in an advancing force needed to overpower a defending force should be in a ratio of 2.5 to 1. This means it would take two and a half million men to overpower a defending force of one million; however, with better intelligence and technology, the ratio becomes obsolete, as demonstrated by the bombing and weakening the Iraqi forces before the ground campaign began in both Iraqi expeditions. Incidentally, application of Deep Battle concepts have produced stunning military accomplishments by U.S. forces in the two Iraqi wars as well as in Afghanistan.

PriorityPath® provides access to the best intelligence available from knowledgeable stakeholders to the betterment of the organization sponsoring the analysis.

M1A1 Abrams Tank

In the mid-eighties, the U.S. Army considered making a block enhancement to the revolutionary M1A1 Abrams tank. Intelligence suggested that existing tank weaponry on the M1A1 Abrams may have difficulty penetrating the new glaciated armor of Soviet-made tanks. The block enhancement they were considering also included the addition of nuclear, biological, and chemical (NBC) protection. The potential barriers to accomplishing these objectives were massive.

Priority Systems® was employed to help assess and bring these barriers under control. The task was to gather and evaluate the issues and risks inherent in such an ambitious undertaking. Participants included designers, manufacturers, tank maintenance crews, the soldiers who would operate the tanks in potentially hazardous conditions, military specialists, and commanders. These people were located both in the United States and on active duty in Europe. Each person contributed his or her judgments about the most critical issues that would be faced in carrying out the block enhancement program.

The analysis highlighted critical areas that needed the greatest amount of attention and, while specific results are still classified, the outcomes of the modifications were very successful. During the course of the analysis, additional weak points of the equipment were identified. During the remediation phase, these additional technical weaknesses were attenuated.

When the United States was involved in the first Iraqi incursion, the threat that the enemy might elect to use biological and chemical weapons became a distinct possibility. The fact that the Abrams tank had been modified to include the NBC system provided welcome security to the soldiers operating the equipment. Where tank battles actually occurred, the Abrams weaponry not only penetrated the Soviet-built tanks, but was able to do so beyond the range of opposing canons on enemy tanks. Both conditions limited the loss of men and equipment.

Priority Systems® provides an important dimension in identifying sources of both real and potential issues and risks before they actually happen. This capability allows savvy management to take preemptive action and avoid the pitfalls and failures that too often surface in the development of complex systems. The experience of avoiding failures in modifying the Abrams Tank is only one example of the benefits that are routinely achieved by using PriorityPath®. Management positions itself in an extraordinarily favorable light when it avoids the potential as well as the real barriers or failures that their associates are capable of identifying.

Army Space Initiative Study (ASIS)

The U.S. Army wanted to explore how space could be used as a combat medium. While the other armed services had a well-defined space doctrine, the Army had not yet developed one. A six-month study was commissioned by the Army to provide a foundation for their use of space. A well-known "Beltway Bandit" consulting firm was awarded the contract—but three months into the study, the lack of consensus and chaos among stakeholders regarding the strategic purpose of the study had produced little that was helpful to the Army. Priority Systems® was awarded a contract to help produce a statement in the remaining three months that would be the basis on which the Army could develop its space doctrine.

The study was being coordinated by personnel at the Army's Fort Leavenworth base. Priority Systems® began its effort by defining the strategic purpose for the study; however, all the stakeholders commissioned to work on the study had differing views on the purpose of the initiative. In order to break the deadlock, all the principal stakeholders were gathered in a single meeting and charged with the responsibility of establishing a strategic purpose statement before the meeting adjourned. The agreement was reached around 3:00 A.M. following nine straight hours of debate.

Once the strategic purpose statement was agreed on, we conducted a typical PriorityPath® analysis. All stakeholders charged with responsibility for developing the Army's use of space concept were interviewed and involved in rank ordering all the input gathered in the interviews. Output profiles were prepared for the various interest groups representing different areas of the Army. These profiles allowed senior Army leaders to see where there was consensus and where there were mismatches; ultimately, many of the mismatches were resolved by building on the areas of consensus. The conclusion of the ASIS study provided the basis for the Army's doctrine for use of space as a combat medium. The Army issued an award to Priority Systems® for our contribution.

New Zealand Defense Forces

New Zealand is the only country in the world, to our knowledge, that insures its military equipment. Priority Systems® was hired to audit their insurance and risk management program. The audit helped the New Zealand Defense Forces (NZDF) and the Audit Branch of the Ministry of Defense (MOD) to assess the effectiveness of the Military Insurance and Risk Management programs in the New Zealand military forces. Military and civilian officials responsible for the program were anxious to determine what changes, if any, needed to be made in order to provide the necessary economic protection from losses that government regulations required.

It became clear from the onset of the analysis that the military, to some degree, had relinquished a portion of its budget authority to the insurance firms. This was demonstrated by actions being taken within the MOD. Recommendations for changes in facilities and operations made by the insurance firms were being implemented in order to improve safety and security. There was concern that premiums for this protection may not have reflected the lowest possible rate.

A PriorityPath® analysis of the Military Insurance and Risk Management program was conducted. Data about the problems, difficulties, and fears associated with the current program were provided by representatives of the military establishment, government overseers, and the insurance companies that carried liability insurance for the military and senior executives.

The data was collected and assembled into the typical cause/effect PriorityPath® diagram. Members of the NZDF administration and representatives of the Navy, Army, Air Force, and involved civilian groups quantified each issue. Reports of the findings were delivered to the client.

At the conclusion of the audit, NZDF initiated remedial action to correct those deficiencies and problems that the analysis determined were priorities. The project focused attention on the components of the insurance program that needed to be improved, allowing it to operate more effectively and efficiently.

C. Petrochemical Industry

Over the past several years, we have conducted eight analyses with the same organization—a company that mines tar sand, separates sand from bitumen, and refines the bitumen to produce synthetic crude oil. On two occasions, when the findings of these separate PriorityPath® projects were implemented, daily cash flows were increased by more than $2 million per day six months earlier than had been expected.

Achieving Rated Capacity

In the first project, the company wanted to set priorities that would help them prevent plugging the slurry system, because plugging caused unplanned or extended shutdowns of the fluidized cokers.

The plant used two large, continuous-process, fluidized cokers—the largest such installations in the world at that time. During the first several months, the cokers had operated at only a fraction of their rated capacity; it seemed that just as one coker started operating, the other plugged—necessitating extensive cleaning, problem analysis, and repeated attempts at starting the unit. After several months of stop-and-go operation, a coker task force was organized to resolve the issues; the task force represented personnel from the manufacturer, the contractor that had installed the units, the company, and expert engineers who had experience with similar systems elsewhere. The task force determined that substantial redesign was probably necessary before the targeted production capacities could be achieved. We said we could help the company prioritize what the task force was considering before they finalized the commitment to redesign.

The task force was particularly interested in determining which of the suggested engineering changes would be most likely to achieve the desired results. We agreed to limit our investigation to the hardware side of the installation—the cokers. But during our first interviews, we quickly realized that many people believed the admitted engineering deficiencies in the cokers could be overcome by more precision in operating them and more care in maintaining them. We asked the managers if they wanted us to include this "softer" data in our analysis. They agreed on the condition that it would not take more time nor cost more money for us to do the analysis. We completed the interviews, then had them rated by the Coker Task Force and selected employees. We immediately noted that for most of the participants, the maintenance and operations issues were of much greater significance than were the hardware/engineering issues.

Some doubts were expressed, and the managers asked that we revise the database to give equal emphasis to both the engineering and management concerns that had been expressed. The second analysis clearly showed considerable support for giving greater emphasis to proper operational procedures and maintenance as a way to contain the engineering deficiencies.

The leader of the Coker Task Force realized that it certainly would be faster and more economical to correct the problems through tighter operational control than it would be to rebuild the cokers. It was determined that new, tighter operational processes would immediately be implemented and that suggested attention to maintenance would also be implemented.

Within a month, the cokers were operating at 85 percent of rated capacity, compared to less than 60 percent that had been the norm before the analysis. While some reengineering of the cokers was necessary, the company was able to postpone those changes to a later, regular shutdown. The company realized significant profits during a time when they would have been denied any revenue if they had proceeded to immediately rebuild the cokers.

Sour Gas Management

Shortly after the coker project, we were involved in a project to reduce the number and severity of incidents involving the release of hydrogen sulfide gas in the company's upgrading facility. Several incidents had resulted in exposure to some employees; although there had been no deaths, both company executives and the government's Occupational Health and Safety Department were highly motivated to reduce the number of exposures and limit the possibility of severely injuring or killing any worker.

The project was overseen by a steering committee made up of supervisors and workers, including some who had actually been exposed to the poison gas. The steering committee formulated an ambitious mission statement that focused attention on developing the processes and procedures that would assure safe operation, making the release of poisonous gases virtually impossible. They directed attention to the engineering aspects of the plant, examining where and how certain areas might be reengineered to overcome design weaknesses and make the operation safer. They also examined operating procedures, capacity for leak detection, adequacy of the alarm system, training, education and awareness programs, and response capability. Every employee in the plant was given an opportunity to respond to the key questions asked in every PriorityPath® project: What is missing? What problems exist that need more attention than they are being given now, and what are the potential problems that you perceive? What is there about this operation that wakes you up at three o'clock in the morning and won't let you go back to sleep?

Interviews were conducted with every available employee working in the refinery. Their responses to the questions were placed in the cause/effect format of a validation diagram; the diagram was posted in the coffee room for several days, and every employee had the chance to help refine the database. New insights were added, the structure was modified, and language was clarified until the result represented all of the issues that refinery employees believed were critical.

The people who had provided data rated the significance of the issues, and the results were presented to management. But because of the urgency of dealing with a major incident elsewhere in the plant, very little about the danger of a gas leak was addressed immediately. As a consequence, the change process was left to the refinery's on-site managers—and, although the managers were preoccupied, plant personnel were extremely interested in making improvements.

Approximately one year later, management again focused on the prevention of sour gas release in the refinery; the Division of Occupational Health and Safety wanted a report on the incidence of sour gas releases and a report of any changes that had been made during the previous year. As managers conducted an assessment of the progress that had been made, they were astounded to learn that the number of releases had declined substantially and that no one had been exposed to sour gas at any time during the previous year. They also noticed another change; the refinery employees now wore protective helmets, fire-resistant clothing, and steel-toed shoes instead of the cowboy hats and casual attire they had previously worn to work.

The changes in practices and attitudes towards safety were so dramatic that oversight by the Occupational Health and Safety Department was relaxed. The organization also mounted a successful Safety and Loss Management program that they successfully marketed to other organizations.

Equipment Startup

Several months later, interest again focused on the cokers. An off-spec connector had been installed by a subcontractor on a service line to a coker, causing a major structural failure that led to a multimillion-dollar fire. The fire consumed the coker, putting it out of operation and necessitating a complete rebuilding of the unit. As the rebuild proceeded, new features of fluidized cokers developed elsewhere were incorporated into the rebuilt structure. The work went according to plan until the plant managers realized that the rebuilt unit, which by now was a combination of both old and new features, was unique. No one had any experience starting up or operating such a unit. Because of the necessity to integrate the old procedures with new ones, the company asked us to help them determine the priorities that must be followed to start the unit and achieve long-term stability of operation. We worked with the designers, installers, supervisors, and operators to examine the priority elements that needed to be observed to secure a viable startup and reasonable run-length of the rebuilt coker.

The scheduled start date for "Oil-In" was at Christmas. In fact, the start date occurred a few days later, in −40° F weather. By following the procedures they had developed and by anticipating and accommodating every negative event that could have interrupted them, they achieved startup in a very short period of time and were able to use the new startup routine as the standard from that time forward. Furthermore, the length of time between major shutdowns for maintenance and cleaning was extended from the previous expectation of eleven to twelve months to twenty-four months.

Project Management Priorities

Some time later the same organization initiated a major expansion project. After the design work had been completed and a managing contractor had been employed, the organization initiated a PriorityPath® program to ensure that the planned expansion program was implemented within cost, schedule, and operability parameters and without negative impact on the reliability of the base plant. The company wanted to make sure that company executives, senior and mid-level managers in the plant, and the managing contractor personnel and subcontractors were properly aligned toward accomplishing their mission. They expected that production of marketable product would be increased. They also wanted to modernize the refinery and alter the processes that would be used.

At the first meeting of the steering committee, members observed that the PriorityPath® project would be fully successful if no deficiencies or problems were discovered. That was a perfectly rational expectation at the outset—the company undertaking the expansion had a reputation for excellence and had employed contractors whose reputations were among the highest in the industry.

We gathered the perceptions of possible hazards, barriers, and difficulties that participants thought could be expected as the construction project progressed. Several hundred issues were noted, most of them relating to possible problems that could occur during the course of the construction program.

When the data was analyzed, executives were interested but not alarmed. There were only a few issues that were of immediate concern, but there were warnings of potential disruptive events that could occur later. The report documents in chart form were placed next to the Pert chart that the managing contractor had prepared to control the project schedule. Both charts were referred to frequently throughout the construction period. As milestone dates were anticipated, executives examined the PriorityPath® chart, noting where potential difficulties had been anticipated. As these expected roadblocks became apparent, the organization took the steps necessary to avoid the potential problems.

During the course of the construction project, three additional PriorityPath® projects were undertaken: integration of new environmental units into the plant, specification of requirements for a state-of-the-art computer control system, and identification of new startup routines.

Environmental Units

Partway through the construction project it was noted that one of the new elements to be added to the plant would have a major impact on the release of gases into the atmosphere. They decided to incorporate a new environmental unit that would facilitate capture of sulfur and minimize the release of sulfur dioxide into the atmosphere. Incorporating the new unit would require a change in the overall chemistry of the plant. There was some debate about the way in which the new unit should be integrated into the existing refinery. A PriorityPath® program was instituted to determine priorities of the designers, builders, and operators so that the probability of creating a totally satisfactory addition would be increased. The judgments of participants were accommodated, the equipment was ordered and installed, and the intended improvements were put in place in the remodeled plant.

Computer Control System

Our second project dealt with concerns that arose about the computer control system that would be used in the expanded refinery. The refinery had started its operations several years earlier using a Taylor manual control system; within three years, plant management decided to upgrade the control system to a Honeywell TDC2000 system. Necessary equipment and programs were purchased and installed, and operations personnel were trained.

The results weren't what the executives had expected. Only about 50 percent of the possible benefits from the TDC2000 system were being realized; other features of the system were simply being ignored.

Eventually, as part of the expansion project, plant management wanted to make sure the plant was using a state-of-the-art control system. Preliminary examination showed that a newly developed Honeywell TDC3000 system would fit their needs, but based on their previous experience with using Honeywell systems, they were extremely concerned that the company would again waste the system's capacity unless the planning and installation phase was conducted more comprehensively than it had been before.

As a result, the company asked Priority Systems® to do a project to make sure that the needs of the plant were fully documented and communicated to Honeywell—and that the plant's operations and technical staff were properly prepared to fully utilize the TDC3000 when it was installed. Our project was conducted before the plant submitted specifications to Honeywell, so the plant was able to clearly indicate what was needed. Our project also outlined areas where training was required and set the framework for effective and timely implementation of the new system.

The TDC3000 system was operational at startup and proved to be very successful, partly because our project and subsequent activities provided early and continuing communication throughout the organization during the planning and installation stages. Not only did the PriorityPath® project prove to be cost effective, it increased commitment and ongoing pride in the workplace as plant personnel realized that the specifications they participated in writing and their preparations for utilization of the system were so successful.

Prior to completion of the expansion project, company executives—noting the challenges they faced in starting the new plant and remembering the work we had done on startup of the cokers—commissioned Priority Systems® to help determine procedures for starting up the new, expanded plant.

Startup of Expansion Plant

There were a number of challenges; the remodeled plant combined old and new features. The preferred plan was to achieve startup of the new units without interfering with ongoing production in the existing plant. Because this meant that a new process was being integrated with ongoing processes, and the chemistry was being altered as the new processes were coming on board, significant opportunities for disruption of the ongoing process were present. There was concern that outages could occur, reducing or totally halting production—events that would have marked effects on overall plant profitability.

As was the case with the coker startup project, we gathered the judgments of operators, maintenance personnel, contractors, supervisors, and executives; the data was formatted, rated for significance, and submitted for assessment and action. Existing procedures were examined in detail, modifications were introduced, and a smooth startup proceeded without significant incidents.

In addition to the projects listed above, we also helped the company reduce the number and severity of incidents that could injure employees or degrade the environment by organizing and implementing a Total Loss Control program. The project mission statement was "To ensure first-class personal safety and reduce the incidents, near misses, and potential threats to the operation, all within the Loss Management Program."

This project led to implementation of a Total Loss Management Program that has been widely copied within the oil and gas industry. Shortly after we finished the project, the company's vice president retired and spent the following ten years teaching and writing scholarly literature that outlined the dimensions of successful loss management in engineering contexts. The priorities ascertained in this PriorityPath® project provided substantial immediate benefits to the organization—and have also been useful to all of the organizations that have adopted the principles advocated in the subsequent research work on loss management.

Rand Corporation Review

Shortly after we finished the plant expansion program, the Rand Corporation published *Understanding the Outcomes of Megaprojects* (Edward W. Merrow, March 1988), a report that examined characteristics of what Rand dubbed *megaprojects*—projects worldwide whose value was in excess of one billion dollars. The plant expansion project we worked on was included in the Rand study. The study found that megaprojects worldwide experience an *average* 88 percent growth in cost and a 17 percent schedule slippage; by understanding the causes behind these, organizations can realize significant savings and make sure that the projects are completed on schedule.

The study also concluded that for megaprojects, the most important correlation between cost growth and schedule slippage is the relationship between project management and the local government. The report highlights the need to "identify the circumstances that lead to regulatory problems and other conflicts between projects and host governments and to avoid or at least mitigate the effects of such problems." The report noted that the plant expansion project with which we were associated did not experience the usual cost overruns—and the plant president indicated that PriorityPath® was a major factor in meeting the company's cost, schedule, and specification objectives.

Loss Management

Eighteen months after conducting an analysis and implementing specific actions to reduce incidents, the company negotiated a 40 percent reduction in insurance premiums with Lloyds of London. The project focused the attention of all employees on the need to implement recommendations that came not only from our analysis, but also from hazard and operability studies, ongoing safety audits, and company training programs. The PriorityPath® process contributed toward changing the culture within the plant, helping employees realize that individual action and constant attention can make significant differences.

In summary, as a result of PriorityPath® projects, output at the plant was substantially increased; startups were routinized; potential hazards were identified, limited, and/or controlled; and environmental compliance was improved in the succession of projects undertaken at the plant. In two instances, cash flow was increased dramatically as equipment was brought online several months earlier than anticipated. The safety and loss control programs that the company formulated with input from our projects are recognized as models in the mining and refinery industries.

Other Petrochemical Installations

Priority Systems® conducted several projects in a similar facility located near the petroleum extraction plant just discussed. The first was implemented to help refinery personnel understand the factors associated with the sour gas it was releasing. Before we conducted our project, the installation experienced an average of one major incident a month that severely injured or killed an employee. As a result, safety had become a major issue in negotiations between management and the union.

Safety

Within one year of completing our project, safety had significantly improved and was no longer an issue in employment contract negotiations. Safety programs were more effective—but, even more important, the unsafe conditions in the plant were repaired. Production and profits improved. Employees became avid supporters of the organization instead of rebelling in fright as they had before our analysis. After the organization implemented the remedial strategies that emanated from our project and from staff members, the major incident rate was reduced from an average of twelve per year to one per year.

Dyke Stabilization

A second project at the same plant centered on stabilizing the dykes that contain effluent from the plant. Some movement in the dykes had raised environmental concerns. Because the dykes are near the banks of a major river that empties into the Arctic Ocean, release of tailings from the plant had the potential to create massive environmental degradation. Our project identified priorities for stabilizing the dykes—and, with appropriate follow-up by the organization, the dykes were stabilized and movement stopped. Fears of an impending environmental incident were greatly reduced.

Sour Gas Management

Projects directed toward controlling the release of sour gas and implementing total loss control have been conducted in several additional petrochemical installations. In one, refinery personnel had routinely used both internal and external personnel to conduct risk assessments to catalog the variety of potentially dangerous conditions, practices, and configurations of equipment that could cause losses. While the lists of issues were impressive, there was no way to determine the priority that should be attached to each risk. It was impossible to determine from the data the likelihood that any of the risks would actually cause a problem—or what order of priority should be attached to each risk. We were able to examine all of the risks they had identified, and using the processes available through the PriorityPath® process, we were able to recommend specific actions, in rank order, that those people whose judgments were of greatest relevance were advising them to take. They were able to capitalize on data that until then had been interesting, but not very action-oriented.

Safety and Loss Management

This approach was extended in a large national oil and gas company that operates numerous facilities. The approach was to determine concerns about safety and loss management from a broad section of employees and executives located in multiple centers across the nation. A database in typical PriorityPath® format was prepared, edited by those who contributed the base information, and rated for relative significance by participants nationwide. The results were then examined by company officials. They determined that a formal loss management program needed to be implemented, and those who conducted the PriorityPath® analysis prepared a draft plan for the corporation. After internal editing, the plan was adopted and remained operational throughout the company for many years.

Two other PriorityPath® projects were conducted for the same company. One was with a plant that extracts ethane gas from natural gas being transported via pipeline from western sources to eastern markets. The ethane contained in the natural gas product was being extracted for processing into ethylene, a highly profitable by-product of the natural gas industry. The first project dealt with repair of turbines and the second focused on recovery of a caisson from a wellhead in the ocean.

Turbine Repair and Operation

Operation of the plant depended on continuous operation of two large gas compression pumps that were powered by large turbines. Unfortunately, the turbines suffered from frequent incidents. When we were engaged to assist them, both turbines were out of commission for the fourth time in eight years. In each case, a rotor blade had been dislodged and thrown through the turbine, tearing up blades and vanes and rendering the turbine inoperable. The company was adamant that the situation had to be addressed fully—not just repaired again. They wanted assurance that all the problems would be addressed completely so the installation would not go down again.

Initial assessment of the situation was made by the contractor who had installed the equipment, the manufacturer, operators, and managers. They soon realized that they probably didn't have the expertise needed to ensure reliable operation. Consequently, they invited a specialty firm that designs rotating equipment and writes textbooks on turbine manufacture and operation to help remedy the situation.

We used a PriorityPath® process to determine what should be done. We spoke with representatives of all the groups mentioned, visited every installation in North America where similar rotating equipment was in operation, and prepared the usual database. The entire participant group edited and modified the database until every participant agreed that it adequately covered all the salient points about reliable operation.

The data was rated for significance using the PriorityPath® process. The results were presented to the contracting company and to representatives of the other participating groups. Decisions were made about the rebuilding, and criteria were generated about operational and maintenance directives and factors that would be considered in ascertaining what would be done if future problems occurred.

Some surprising results also emerged. As just one example, the manufacturer, trainers, and supervisors all knew that when a critical red RPM indicator light came on, the turbine was operating at design speed. We learned, however, that there was an informal understanding among the operators that the red light indicated that the turbine must be running too fast. The operators typically responded by cutting back the RPMs to slow the machine down. They didn't realize that slowing the turbine generated dangerous vibrations that were dislodging blades, throwing the blades through the turbine, and destroying the equipment. Once this was identified, the color of the indicator light was changed from red to green, the more universal color of safe operation.

Caisson Recovery Problem

The final project with this company was directed toward a highly technical problem experienced in a deep-sea drilling program in the Hibernia Oil Field off the coast of Newfoundland. A particular well was drilled by a drilling ship. Tests revealed that potential flows from the well would be commercially viable, and arrangements were made to finish the well. By law, the well had to be drilled in an excavation into the sea floor. Because the ocean floor in that area is at a relatively shallow depth, and because very large icebergs routinely pass through the area, a well head on the ocean floor could easily be torn off by an iceberg scraping along the bottom, releasing oil freely into the water. Such an environmental incident could not be tolerated, which explains the legal necessity to drill from an excavation into the sea floor. The drilling company used a caisson attached to the drill head, extending upward to create an artificial well head at approximately the level of the sea floor, from which to do the actual drilling.

When the well was completed, the drilling company and the crew of the drilling ship had to remove the caisson. Their plan was to turn the caisson through several degrees, breaking the seal and lifting the caisson to the surface. When they tried, however, they found that the caisson was stuck and couldn't be rotated; they had to come up with an alternate plan.

They identified several options: (1) abandon the well—cement it, seal it, and leave everything in place; (2) spend hundreds of thousands of dollars to try other equipment to dislodge and remove the caisson; or (3) convert the well to an injection well, limiting its economic value and writing off the considerable funds they had spent to complete it. Obviously, none of the options was particularly attractive.

We used the PriorityPath® process to sort out the alternatives, to disclose every factor that people involved in all aspects of the drilling activity believed was relevant, and to provide direction for managers as they prepared recommendations and a rationale for action. Their final decision continues to be a confidential matter.

Property Services

A few months after a large petrochemical company formed a Property Services Division to manage its real property, a new vice president of the division was appointed. He quickly realized that the services his division provided were not valued by the people using them, so he asked for a PriorityPath® project to examine those services.

When our analysts conducted confidential interviews with the various stakeholders, we found why there were negative perceptions; we then compiled and formatted the information into a useful diagram. Participants edited the diagram to make sure it was exhaustive and complete, the data was quantified, and we provided project results to company management and to all those who participated. Goodwill was fostered as participants saw concrete evidence that they were being heard.

The results of our project led to the amalgamation of division functions into the basic structure of the organization, which in turn resulted in increased support from the user groups. The vice president indicated that without the PriorityPath® analysis he may have spent years instead of weeks accomplishing the same result. As an added bonus, our project helped him in a very short time get acquainted with and oriented to the property management issues facing the organization.

Alberta Energy Resources Conservation Board (ERCB): Three Projects

1. Pincher Creek Project

For more than twenty years, some residents of the Pincher Creek area in the sparsely populated and scenic foothill country of Southwestern Alberta living downwind from two sour gas processing plants had tried unsuccessfully to determine whether emissions from the plants were causing illness. Shortly after consecutive startups in the mid-fifties, horror stories began circulating about sudden unexplained farm animal miscarriages, deformities, color changes in paint, corrosion of barbed wire fences, and serious health effects on residents—including increased respiratory illnesses and an apparent increase in the number of deaths attributable to cancer. At the very least, it seemed that the pristine beauty of the area was being irreparably damaged.

Action was taken by the companies to limit the release of sour gas. Wells were no longer permitted to vent to the atmosphere. Control of emissions from the processing plants received priority attention. However, there was still a perception among many in the downwind communities that their health was being affected. They were also concerned that property values were being depressed.

After several years, studies with limited mandates were conducted to address the controversial illness and environmental factors. However, nothing conclusive resulted from these. Sides were taken, disagreements were becoming more vigorous, and the news media was typically fomenting dissent. The Energy Resources Conservation Board (ERCB) turned to Priority Systems® to determine the direction that would lead to resolution of these very public issues.

Following a presentation by Priority Systems® to the primary groups that were eventually included in the project, there was much debate about what could be accomplished, with the greatest reservations being expressed by the Public Advisory Committee of the Environment Council of Alberta. All those concerned agreed to go ahead with the PriorityPath® project only after being assured that the steering committee would have a representative from each of their significantly divergent viewpoints—the two gas plants, general environment, medicine, chemistry, engineering, education, meteorology, biochemistry, toxicology, veterinary science, agriculture, and civic government.

After considerable discussion, the steering committee formulated the following mission statement as an expression of what they hoped to achieve

Appendix D • Project Summaries   147

through the PriorityPath® analysis:

To achieve improved health and well-being in the area by identifying the nature and origins of health problems, neither limiting nor excluding the origins to the adjacent natural resources development projects.

The analysts attended numerous community meetings, interviewed representatives selected by the steering committee from each interest group, drew up the PriorityPath® diagram in typical format, ensured that participants validated the information, assisted some 195 people to rate the relative significance of each issue, reported back to the steering committee and the interest groups, and assisted the steering committee to formulate and implement recommendations.

Once we knew the priorities of the various groups, we reported them and captured suggestions on how each major issue could be addressed. Among many findings, the steering committee established to their collective satisfaction that there was not enough scientific evidence about the extent and effects of air and water pollution emanating from the plant to make informed decisions about the impacts (if any) on the health of residents.

As a result of steering committee recommendations, the Alberta government authorized an epidemiological study to be conducted by McGill University, Montréal. At a cost of more than $3.4 million, this medical study was hailed as the most comprehensive work of its type ever conducted in Canada. In addition, the Engineering Department of the University of Waterloo was asked to monitor stack emissions from the plants at selected distances downwind over the next eighteen months.

Oil company executives have said that they do not believe that the two studies would have been authorized or financed if the PriorityPath® project had not first set the climate. Concerned residents were satisfied that they had been heard and that the issues had been addressed in the best possible way.

The McGill findings did not point conclusively to unusual health problems in the area, nor did they implicate the gas processing plants. The incidence of illness and symptoms downwind from the two plants was indistinguishable from those being experienced by two control groups living in areas where gas processing plants were not located. The Waterloo studies indicated that the concentrations of emissions from the plants were below recognized standards that define pollution of the air.

While there continue to be questions, all parties agreed that everything was done that could have been done to provide valid answers. The chairman of the ERCB said that his expectations were exceeded in the project.

2. Hewitt Oil Processing Plant

Hewitt Oil faced significant community opposition to its proposal to build a small processing plant in a semi-urban area just west of Edmonton, Alberta. It owned three old natural gas wells that were beginning to produce more hydrogen sulfide gas than the company that was processing their natural gas would accept. It became necessary to either abandon the wells or take action to remove the sour gas so the product could continue to be marketed.

Hewitt examined several alternatives and eventually decided to construct a small sour gas processing facility using an innovative process to "sweeten" its product. Engineering was completed and plans were made to proceed with the construction. At this point, it became necessary by law for the company to inform the public of the development plans. Since the project was very small, they thought that informing the public would be more of a formality than a problem. Consequently, notice of a public meeting to discuss the proposed new plant was issued in the press, flyers and public notices were distributed and exhibited as the law prescribed, and company executives convened the required meeting.

Instead of the few inquisitive residents that had been anticipated, the small community hall was packed with people who stated energetically that they absolutely did not want a sour gas processing plant in their back yard. With the vigorous opposition that had materialized, there was considerable concern that required approval of the Energy Resources Conservation Board (ERCB) would not be given.

ERCB had worked with us on previous projects, so ERCB officers advised Hewitt Oil to explore the possibility of using our process to help them communicate their intent to the community. We were eventually hired to help make sure that effective communication would occur between and among the industry, community groups, and various local and provincial regulatory agencies involved in approving the project.

Our project educated local residents about many aspects of the oil and gas industry. We clearly set out the legal requirements, discussed the nature of environmental protection that existed, and explored every objection that individuals and groups had to the Hewitt project.

When the results were tabulated, it became apparent that greater attention needed to be paid to ensuring that the public was informed through thorough communications programs. Following our project, formal lines of communication were established, the expressed priorities of residents were implemented, the construction was completed, and subsequent operation and cooperation has been exemplary. The project was also accepted as meeting the requirements of a formal environmental assessment. In the year following completion of the new facility, Hewitt Oil was given an award as the most environmentally responsible operator in the province for its success in planning, building, and operating the Hewitt Parkland Plant.

3. City of Calgary Emergency Response Plan Modification

The City of Calgary sits on a pool of natural gas that contains approximately 36 percent hydrogen sulfide, an extremely poisonous gas that must be removed before the gas can be exported to North American markets or used for either residential or industrial purposes locally. Producing, processing, and distributing this sour gas are major industries in Calgary.

When an oil company proposed to drill a sour gas well within one mile of the Calgary city boundaries, public opposition was immediate. People were also alarmed when they discovered that more than thirty such wells were already located in the same general area. A consultant had estimated on the basis of conservative projections that, under certain conditions, a release of gas had the potential to poison many residents of the city. Making matters worse, people found out that the city's emergency response plan did not contain specific provisions for helping the public in the event of a sour gas release.

We were hired by the ERCB to work with residents, city emergency crews, petrochemical experts, and local and provincial government regulators to determine what changes were needed in the city's emergency response plan to make it fully effective in its response to an accidental release of sour gas in or near the city. After we released our project findings, the steering committee—including personnel from City of Calgary Emergency Services—produced, tested, and adopted a plan that outlines procedures to be followed in case of a sour gas release. The plan was accepted by the public but is under continuous revision as new threats are identified.

A Major Resource Company: Offshore Drilling

A major international resources company retained Priority Systems® to identify and prioritize the risks associated with drilling for oil in the Beaufort Sea, near Alaska off the northern shore of Canada in the Arctic Ocean. The focus of the project was to discover every factor that could limit the company's probable success in finding, producing, marketing, and distributing the light crude oil that exists in abundance in this area below the Beaufort Sea. Another major focus was to ascertain risks and help determine procedures that would be effective in preventing the occurrence of an environmental incident during the drilling phase of the exploration activity.

We met with management personnel in the offices of the company and with service personnel and employees actually working on the offshore drilling rigs. Participants were asked to identify existing problems, potential problems, and elements that they believed were missing in the drilling program. Priorities were calculated for each participating group, and the results were fed back to company principals.

After careful review, remedial actions were planned and implemented. These remedial activities helped limit costs, prevent risks to personnel, and improve processes for avoiding environmental degradation. When a non-preventable incident actually occurred on one of their rigs just after the PriorityPath® project was completed, the actions that were generated by implementing project findings were instrumental in securing the safety of personnel and limiting the impact of the incident. Although the movement of ice onto an artificial island caused significant erosion and dropped some equipment into the sea, no individual was at risk at any time. Had this occurred before action had been taken on the results of our project, company officials estimated that lives may very well have been lost.

The company project manager suggested that if a similar project directed toward limiting the negative impacts of human decisions had been conducted with respect to transporting oil in tankers in the Gulf of Alaska, the Exxon-Valdez incident probably could have been avoided.

D. GOVERNMENT AND REGULATORY AGENCY PROJECTS

Traffic Management/Bay of Fundy

The marine organization responsible for safe transport of people and goods in the Bay of Fundy off the coasts of Maine, New Brunswick, and Nova Scotia was limited in its capacity to monitor the shipping corridor and provide constant oversight to shipping, recreational, and passenger traffic in the Bay. Radar coverage had been provided for most of the area, but there were blind areas behind islands where radar could not detect ships and boats. The situation was complicated by the daily traffic of large oil tankers—some with single hulls—that were transporting crude oil to the many refineries located near seaports on the Bay. Another complication was the monstrous tides, up to forty feet in height, that flood the bay twice a day.

There was genuine concern that this combination of conditions posed a significant threat to all classes of shipping. Officials were afraid that a situation with potentially dangerous and costly environmental impacts may occur at any time without warning in these international waters. Flooding the pristine U.S. and Canadian beaches that line the Bay of Fundy with crude oil was an environmental threat that no one could accept. Furthermore, the danger of collisions and the resulting unnecessary loss of life were also unthinkable and intolerable.

The agency with the mandate to secure safety of Bay of Fundy traffic knew they needed to buy, install, and operate additional equipment—but it was having difficulty preparing a convincing case for the government budgeting office that would provide the funds it needed. The request for funding also needed to be accompanied by a comprehensive analysis of all the factors associated with safe operation of shipping and recreational boating in the Bay.

Priority Systems® was engaged to conduct the safety analysis. Analysts interviewed personnel from the responsible agency as well as people from the overseeing government department, executives from companies that were transporting oil in the Bay, refinery operators, and a selection of people who frequently engaged in sports boating and sailing in the Bay. We prepared a database of every issue relevant to safety. We then had the participants validate it and rate it for relative significance.

Profiles of the priorities of all participating groups were made available to the appropriate officials, and actions were taken to overcome the priority problems that became apparent in the analysis. One major change involved the revision of safety regulations for shipping and vessel traffic in the Bay, providing greater assurance for the safety of all vessels. The results of the project also led to funding and installation of additional radar equipment. With full radar coverage and increased attention to safe operation by all parties that navigate the Bay, a major incident is not nearly as likely to occur as before the results of the safety improvement project were implemented.

Airport Safety and Security

The same federal government department is also responsible for safety and security policies and practices on airports. The department initiated a PriorityPath® analysis to conduct a major examination of issues surrounding maintenance of safety, including prevention of crashes, sabotage, fire, and provision of rescue services on airport property throughout the nation. The study involved all the major air carriers, associations of airline employees, and aircraft manufacturers in Canada.

The project was performed in association with a consulting company that specializes in airport design and operation with clients throughout the world.

They were able to arrange contact with senior officials in each of the participating groups. Ninety individuals contributed 466 issues relating to political, policy, and planning factors; human resource utilization; operational procedures; and adequacy of equipment, facilities, and materials used to ensure that crash, firefighting, and rescue services were available and being used optimally.

Most of the ninety people who supplied information participated in rating the relative significance of the issues. Priorities of the differing groups were compiled and reported back to the representatives of interest groups that guided the analysis project.

The results were reported in a three-volume document that was examined by department officials. Over the next few months, actions were taken by both the government and participating organizations to address many of the priorities that emerged. The result was that safety on and in the vicinity of airports has been improved.

A Workers' Compensation Board

The chairman of a Workers' Compensation Board inherited a $200 million deficit when he was appointed to office; four years later, he suddenly discovered that the deficit had escalated to more than $600 million during his chairmanship. His sense of surprise was compounded by the fact that his executives had not warned him about this extraordinary situation.

The chairman asked Priority Systems® to perform an organizational assessment into what caused the problem and to help generate recommendations for the future. To begin, we interviewed representatives from each division of the Workers' Compensation Board along with major clients and government regulators. They responded with insights about the factors that had caused the deficit and what needed to be done to make sure that the organization would be successful in the future. In meetings with the new executive team, plans based on the insights and priorities of participants were formulated and immediately implemented.

Initially, rates for compensation coverage had to be increased. This, of course, was not popular with clients, but because they had participated in assessing and prioritizing the direction that the board needed to follow to become solvent, they reluctantly accepted the rate increases.

The change in rate structure and a program focused on cost reductions helped the organization fully recover the deficit within twenty-three months. By continuing the same policies, the board posted an $80 million surplus within the following year. At this point, rates were adjusted to a level that was among the lowest in North America. Executives of the Workers' Compensation Board recognized that the strategic direction discovered through the Priority Systems® project together with the decisive actions taken by the board and its executives were instrumental in the success.

Coordination of OH&S Services

As we worked with the board, it was noted that claims for compensation were closely interrelated with programs emanating from the associated Occupational Health and Safety agency. Because of the high degree of interest in getting better control over claims, we were asked to help improve the coordination and delivery of occupational health programs by the Workers' Compensation Board and the Department of Labor. Our purpose was to ensure that the activities of each agency were congruent with and supportive of the initiatives of workers, employers, and allied safety associations.

Our analysis focused on governance issues, core activities, and the nature of support being given to these core activities. We also examined the impact of external forces on OH&S. Again, we contacted individuals and agencies within the industry, their associations, and the allied regulatory bodies. Our analysis determined that a greater emphasis needed to be placed on long-term planning and that there was a need to de-politicize OH&S activities by increasing the emphasis on collaborative policy making. As a result, some impediments to good working relationships were identified and addressed. We also found that more emphasis needed to be placed on preventing and reducing illnesses and injuries instead of just looking at monetary implications and effects.

The improved coordination among agencies was one of the major changes that led to the significant improvement of the total OH&S program that occurred.

Government Departments

Recreation and Parks Department

At a time when almost all government revenues were shrinking, a Recreation and Parks agency determined that it should initiate programs to limit expenditures while providing excellent services before an external mandate dictated that reductions must immediately be made.

To start, the department examined its organizational structure. In compliance with overall government policy, the department had begun to regionalize many of its activities—but a number of people in the administrative division of the department believed that a return to more centralized control might achieve the desired budget-limiting effects.

Not everyone in the department agreed—nor did the senior government leaders. Consequently, the department determined that it needed to do an assessment that would include every possible way to limit expenditures while providing exemplary services. Priority Systems® was engaged to help in the assessment.

We interviewed people from every part of the department, examined their differences in judgments, and structured all of their responses into an integrated database diagram. The people who had been interviewed then determined the relative severity of each of the issues they had identified.

The results showed that the vast majority of people in the department believed that the operations should be regionalized to the greatest extent possible and that money would be saved as decisions were delegated to the lowest possible level in the hierarchy. The resulting changes were made rather rapidly and were accepted both within the department and by the public that was receiving services. The department was able to retain all its programs without an increase in user fees while reducing both actual costs and personnel by 15 percent.

Several months later, central government announced that during the following week every department needed to outline how it would meet stringent new guidelines on expenditures. The department we had worked with met with the government's budget department immediately, presented the plan that had been based on our analysis, and received instant endorsement. Later that same day, we received a phone call from the senior budget officer for the government, who asked that we show him precisely what we had done.

A Sister Department

We responded, and found him very receptive to our approach. He then told us about another department that needed to perform a similar analysis. We did the requested analysis, but were not met with the same enthusiasm as in the Recreation and Parks agency; when we presented results of our analysis, the senior leader expressed interest but told us that elected officials in the department would soon be changed. He delayed implementation of any changes pending arrival of the new leadership.

We heard little about developments in his department until eighteen months later. During a phone call, we learned that the second department *had* undergone some critical changes—but because our recommended budget-reducing activity had not taken place, senior government officials had arbitrarily taken over financial management. To regain control of the budget, they dismissed a sizable number of career employees. Furthermore, public access to their services was severely restricted, and the public had to pay fees to use facilities that had formerly been provided without charge. The senior budget officer observed that had the second department implemented our findings as had the first department, the radical external restrictions probably would not have been necessary.

Wildlife Management

Public dissatisfaction with the management of wildlife—and particularly big game—became a major concern after the fall hunting season in a western Canadian province. Public expression of dissatisfaction began immediately after hunting season ended as wildlife officers culled herds of deer, elk, moose, and other game animals—culling that was made necessary because the habitat in which the game lived would not support the increasing population of animals that lived there. Had the culling not been carried out, many animals would have starved or, at the very least, experienced illnesses that would compromise the long-term survival of the wildlife population. People who had competed for hunting licenses were incensed that the game they wanted to harvest during the hunting season was being disposed of in a way that violated the interests of hunters, conservationists, animal rights activists, and the general public.

For some time, informal discussions had been held with government officials and a broad cross section of interest groups about alternative ways to manage the big game resource. As a result of these discussions, we were invited to conduct a comprehensive analysis of all the factors that would be associated with alternate means of managing big game.

A mission statement expressing the need for new direction was written, and representatives of every involved interest group were interviewed to ascertain their concerns and to receive their recommendations about what should be done to improve management of big game. Those groups included government policy makers and regulators, the Metis and Indian associations, guides and outfitters associations, the Sierra Club, sports writers and broadcasters, and many people who had expressed interest in changing the current system.

When the priorities of the participating groups were made available to government personnel, the results were translated into a white paper format.

The document contained all of the critical issues associated with making changes and outlined several ways to change the big game management program.

After the white paper had been circulated for several months, legislation outlining new regulations was introduced. A major change was the introduction of legislation that permitted big game ranching. Until then, it was a major offense to hold wildlife captive; new legislation made it legal to capture a certain number of animals and raise them in the same way livestock is raised on ranches.

The result of all this activity was the development of a new rural industry in the province. Deer and elk are now raised on ranches, and hunters are given periodic opportunities to harvest selected animals. A profitable business serving big game entrees has evolved, giving many restaurants an opportunity to expand their businesses into this exotic new field. Culling of herds is no longer necessary. The natural habitat has been preserved, and many more animals exist in an area where they previously were becoming endangered species.

Department of Environment

Development of the oil industry in Alberta had produced a situation in both rural and urban areas where remnants of industrial installations were still part of the landscape. These included abandoned oil and gas wells located indiscriminately on private property, similar situations on public land, and sites of various sizes within municipalities where industrial relics prevented use of the sites for other purposes. The risks of environmental pollution of the landscape and potential health hazards to residents were real.

Systems were in place for reclaiming these sites, but the cumbersome nature of existing regulations did not encourage such reclamation. Interest was great in resolving the issue. Residents, local officials, and government officials were anxious to move forward, while representatives of industry were anxious to ensure that costs of cleaning sites were kept to a minimum.

Priority Systems® worked with Alberta Environment Department, industry personnel, former industrial users, and land owners to determine and prioritize components of an acceptable new land reclamation plan. Our work, based on input from those who knew the situation, resulted in redrafting of the relevant regulations. Specifically, the project helped determine priority actions for returning land that had been used for industrial purposes to regular domestic use.

Department of Justice Project

The Department of Justice in a large Canadian province wanted to examine the adequacy of the court system that serviced its largest metropolitan community. The involved city is located adjacent to a large body of water, creating the common problem that similarly situated urban communities experience: street access to the central core is available from only one side, because there is water on the other side.

In this city, most of the court buildings were located near the city center. Prisons, however, were located some distance away on the city fringes. This geographic separation of institutions whose purposes are interconnected created substantial logistical problems. Transportation of prisoners housed in facilities on the outskirts of the city was becoming both time-consuming and increasingly expensive; those who had to be transported for court appearances during peak hours routinely left for court before 4:00 A.M., placing considerable burdens on support personnel. Furthermore, additional court space was needed, and there was considerable debate about where the court facilities should be located.

Some suggestions for remedying the problem had already been made. Among them was the idea that less egregious offenses could be delegated to the lower courts. It was also suggested that smaller court facilities could be built closer to the prisons. Many legal, political, and logistical viewpoints accompanied every suggestion.

In the midst of the arguments, the Department of Justice engaged Priority Systems® to help analyze conditions and provide a list of priorities of the various groups that would be affected by any decision. Interviews were held with Provincial Justice Department personnel, corrections officers, city and provincial police, and other civic leaders. They provided their judgments about what must be done, what problems needed to be corrected, and their concerns about conditions that were developing.

The steering committee used the priorities of the various participating groups to formulate a strategic plan for future development of the court system. Ultimately it was determined that relocating court facilities was a wise decision, and new facilities were both built and leased to better meet the needs of the community.

A Government Shared Services Project

In one situation, a Canadian provincial government department that provides shared services to all other government departments used PriorityPath® to set priorities for the way it interacts with other departments. To begin, we contacted 985 people from ten stakeholder groups that represented all elements of the departmental workforce and its customers in the other departments they serve. These participants listed additional services that should be provided, reviewed critical problems they were experiencing, and expressed concerns about future issues they feared could frustrate delivery of needed services.

We formatted the resulting information into PriorityPath® charts that were validated by representatives from each of the departments. After duplicate items were removed and new ideas were added, the diagram outlined almost 400 issues that hundreds of people believed needed to be addressed. We put the edited database on the Internet; almost 500 people logged in, rated the items for relative significance, specified their degree of knowledge about each issue, and indicated how difficult or easy they believed it would be to resolve each issue. The results showed precisely what the critical issues were and what differences and similarities existed in the way shared services should be delivered within each department.

The department used the results of the analysis to develop a performance management and accountability framework to ensure that corporate strategy would be translated into action at all levels; consistent with their value proposition of customer intimacy, the framework was based on capturing the strategic objectives of the organization within the context of a *balanced scorecard*. This enabled all managers and employees to selectively target the needs of the customer, the financial implications of programs and services, the processes that support business, and the capacity of the organization to grow and develop. These objectives were in turn used as the drivers for change and action at the business unit and individual levels.

Referencing strategic objectives, performance indicators were established in consultation with the customer and were used collectively to compile a *business-specific, weighted performance index*. These strategic objectives framed the business objectives and performance indicators for each line of business, which were negotiated with the customer and put into a weighted performance index. This index was used as a monitoring and evaluation tool and as an aid to continuous improvement.

Considerable interest in this approach to generating performance standards that are tied to the current realities within an organization has been shown by many other groups that have observed the work of this department.

Industrial Safety

An Occupational Safety and Health regulatory agency used the PriorityPath® process to limit the incidence and severity of injuries in three industries.

A Mine

The first was a large mining operation; the nature of mine work creates conditions leading to frequent back injuries. To begin, we met with a panel of mine workers, managers, and supervisors, and we asked them what major factors needed to be addressed to reduce the injury rate. We reviewed results with a steering committee whose task was to generate specific recommendations for improvement. Specialists from the regulatory agency that sponsored the project assisted in this work.

The recommendations were implemented. Specific prevention programs and publicity heightened awareness among the miners; in addition, managers focused on injury prevention, engaged in closer supervision, and provided improved technical assistance. Over the next four years, the back injury accident rate in the mine declined by 40 percent, resulting in significant savings in lost days, manpower replacement, and Workers' Compensation and insurance premiums. Both the mine management and the regulatory agency recognized that the PriorityPath® process played a significant role in those accomplishments.

The benefit wasn't restricted to prevention of back injuries; project managers at the mine indicate that the number of all types of incidents has decreased significantly. That's because the culture had changed. It used to seem impossible to fund any type of program to reduce injuries; the cooperative PriorityPath® approach, however, created plant-wide agreement to integrate maintenance and incident-reduction spending. As a result, employee suggestions for physical changes in the plant now achieve priority status in budgets—and they are implemented. Staff members, seeing this commitment to physical change, exercise greater care in all assigned tasks. The resulting reduction in insurance and Workers' Compensation premiums is significant.

A Hospital

A similar project was conducted in a large urban hospital under the auspices of the same Occupational Health and Safety organization. Before we were involved, an average of five employees left work early every day with some degree of back strain or injury from slipping on wet floors, lifting patients without adequate assistance or equipment, and performing other routine hospital staff activities.

Our analysis prioritized the judgments of the hospital workers ranging from nurses to nursing assistants, doctors, administrators, and janitorial staff. The consensus was that the hospital needed to pay more attention to incident prevention. People knew that patients would have to be lifted and moved whether help was available or not—a situation that was producing preventable strains and more serious back injuries. Furthermore, it was noted that the hospital did not have access to a sufficient number of mechanical patient lifters.

The report of priorities was presented to management; over time, many of the issues were addressed to the satisfaction of the employees through changes in expectations and awareness programs that focused on prevention.

Safety in the Oil Fields

A number of years ago, the oil drilling industry in western Canada was plagued by an unusual and inordinate number of injuries and accidents. In one province, thirteen deaths were recorded in a single year, and many more lost-time incidents occurred. Public pressure mounted; the press and citizenry called on the government to intervene, change regulations, and slow the injury rate.

Priority Systems® submitted a proposal to government to conduct an analysis that would determine causes of deaths and incidents and generate recommendations for necessary change.

In addition to interviewing numerous oil patch executives, we visited fifty-nine drilling and well-servicing rigs, where we interviewed managers, supervisors, regulatory agency personnel, and roughnecks about what they thought caused the high incident rates. We then formatted and edited the information and participants rated it for significance. We assembled profiles of the priorities for all participating groups, presented them to representatives of each group, and used them to generate specific recommendations on how to improve safety for oil field workers.

The final report was widely distributed and became a standard for drilling companies committed to improving safety practices. Several years later, a group of organizations representing all aspects of the oil and gas industry reviewed the findings of the original report. They declared that our recommendations remained viable, and they advocated greater inspection and enforcement of regulations that came out of the original work as a way to achieve an even better standard of safety.

A Major Housing Authority

Two projects were conducted with a major housing authority in a Midwestern city in the United States. The first project assessed conditions and wrote a strategic plan for the city's housing authority, one of forty authorities in urban areas that were on the federal government's Troubled Cities List.

As a direct result of following the strategic action plan that we wrote with them, the housing authority was removed from the Troubled Cities List and given a $50 million grant from the federal government in recognition of their success. PriorityPath® analysis has been given public recognition for the part it contributed toward this accomplishment.

We also assessed the adequacy and management of the same housing authority's Section 8 program. To begin, our analysts met with the project steering committee and introduced our methodology; the steering committee then determined the specific direction the project would follow. After several meetings, the mission statement was adjusted to read as follows:

> *To administer an alternative housing program for participants which provides greater flexibility in meeting their housing needs through utilization of geographically dispersed, rent subsidized, privately owned housing units.*

Embodied within the mission statement were the following components:

- Complying fully with all legislative, HUD, and authority regulatory requirements
- Increasing opportunities for the economic development of participants
- Fostering a more broadly dispersed community involvement opportunity to help meet the social needs of participants
- Meeting the reasonable and legitimate interests of housing unit providers
- Ensuring that landlords supply quality housing that meets or exceeds adopted Section 8 standards
- Creating a closer association among the authority's conventional, Section 8, and Home Ownership housing programs
- Serving Section 8 stakeholders in a way that recognizes the dignity of beneficiaries, demonstrates respect for them as individuals, and shows sensitivity to their needs

- Strengthening the Section 8 housing option by:
  (a) seeking maximum utilization of funding opportunities;
  (b) recognizing, empowering, and assisting staff to be responsive in administering Section 8 programs;
  (c) incentivizing positive landlord performance; and
  (d) improving the quality of life of participants.

The mission statement and its attendant goals became the focal point for all project activities. Once the steering committee specified the scope and direction of the project, we interviewed a sample of people involved in Section 8—including Section 8 employees, tenants, and landlords. The resulting information was formatted into a cause/effect diagram that illustrated in a graphic way the areas that participants believed were in need of attention. These issues were then rated for significance, and profiles of priority were calculated for each participating group. The results were reported back to the authority, which subsequently planned intervention activities.

The authority organized quality action teams to address the priority issues that were disclosed by the analysis. Each of the five teams focused on analyzing details with respect to the priority theme it was addressing and generating specific recommendations. Priority themes included:

- Analysis of the functions of program analysts, program assistants, and financial analysts—including work flow analysis—and recommendations regarding structure(s) necessary to secure appropriate housing and place qualified applicants into the units.
- Consideration of the merits of constructing a checklist that would accompany files transferred from group to group in support of contract creation. The team also looked at what should be kept in files and considered ways of rationalizing and accomplishing reasonable production standards.
- How to make sure that the needs and concerns of section staff would be fully considered as decisions were made to improve file systems, including a possible move to electronic filing.
- How to improve facilities at the Section 8 offices.
- Actions Section 8 personnel should take to meet the concerns of external people.

Through these teams, *every* employee was given the opportunity to participate on a team, to voice opinions about issues, to help explore possible solutions, and to help formulate and present recommendations. Priority

Systems® analysts were made available to help train the teams and act as coaches in making the teams effective.

The project resulted in substantial changes to the management structure, relationships with residents and landlords, and the introduction and continuation of total quality management within the housing authority. It also resulted in a request to conduct similar analyses and introduce quality improvement activities in each of the five regional administrative sections of the housing authority.

Tauranga District Council

One of the fastest growing communities on New Zealand's North Island, Tauranga is a beautiful coastal city on the west side of North Island with quaint shops and a mild climate. With a change to the local government act in 1989, cities and boroughs throughout New Zealand were encouraged to amalgamate to minimize administrative costs. As a result, Tauranga merged with Mount Maunganui Borough Council and incorporated Papamoa, a small area of the Western Bay of Plenty, to form the Tauranga District Council.

The amalgamation meant that the new Tauranga District Council now had two separate water supply systems that needed to be integrated. The situation was complicated by the fact that the Mount Maunganui Borough Council area had water meters, while the Tauranga and Papamoa areas did not. The Tauranga District Council eventually decided that all connections to their water supply should be metered to preserve water quality and address the ever-increasing demand for water. The mayor, city council, and administrators wanted all residents to be treated fairly, so they came up with a plan to install water meters in the Tauranga and Papamoa areas. Until then, these citizens had enjoyed unlimited water usage for a modest fixed water rate.

The citizens that would be affected by the plan formed a Water Action Group to vigorously oppose the installation of water meters. The action group was financed by a wealthy landowner determined at all costs to avoid restrictions on his water usage, and their actions were causing the council a great deal of consternation and expense.

Tauranga was familiar with Priority Systems® from an earlier study, and it wanted to use PriorityPath® to look at all the issues and risks involved in uniformly installing water meters on all residences within the council boundaries. We conducted our analysis in the usual way, with issues and risks gathered from all stakeholders—including the Water Action Group.

We placed the stakeholder-supplied information into a database, and our analysts formatted it into an easy-to-review cause/effect diagram that was reviewed by the stakeholders who had contributed the information. Their review ensured the information was accurate, exhaustive, and complete.

As the Water Action Group reviewed the diagram, the wealthy sponsor indicated that the process had neutralized the group's concerns. When asked what he meant by "neutralize," he indicated that all the issues raised by the group had been captured by the analysis—and that the city's actions to address these issues would leave them without any justification for their opposition to the installation of water meters. Incidentally, that's precisely what the council accomplished; all the residents of Tauranga District Council now have water meters.

The ability of PriorityPath® to gather the issues and risks facing a project and to treat them with dignity and respect helps resolve complex issues, including those raised by grassroots community organizations like those in Tauranga.

Gisborne District Council (GDC)

PriorityPath® often helps resolve particularly thorny issues between city governments and the public. This is what happened in the New Zealand city of Gisborne. Gisborne is located on North Island's east coast and is known for its agricultural products and local surfboarding. World surfing championships have been held there, and local surf shops display the names and signatures of some of the greatest names in surfing. Gisborne is also famous for being the first city in the world to see the sun at the beginning of the new millennium, which was occasioned by a huge country-wide celebration sponsored by the Gisborne District Council, or GDC.

Gisborne needed a new solid waste landfill—the existing landfill had reached its maximum capacity. Solid waste landfill sites are difficult to establish because of the negative environmental impacts they produce. Increased traffic, offensive odors, unsightliness, and impacts on property values are other factors that arise. Everyone agrees they are necessary, but people generally want them to be placed in someone else's "patch." Gisborne had selected a primary site for the new landfill, and the people who would experience the greatest impact from the site selection had organized an opposition campaign.

PriorityPath® was used to identify the issues and risks, including those raised by the opposition, that stood in the way of successfully establishing the proposed landfill. This analysis gave the GDC insight into the substantive risks, environmental concerns, and arguments of the opposition. Armed with this information, the council and staff were able to make factually based decisions about viable alternative methods of waste disposal and to use these alternatives rather than rush into constructing the proposed landfill.

PriorityPath® helped the council avoid the serious problems—including lengthy litigation—that almost certainly would have occurred had it developed the originally chosen site. By using the alternative, the GDC gained time to explore additional solutions to the environmental issues they identified. Many alternatives are still open to them, including moving forward with plans to develop the initially targeted site.

Hastings City Council

A beautiful city located in the southwest part of New Zealand's North Island, Hastings has many quaint shops and fine restaurants—but, like many cities in New Zealand, Hastings is experiencing population growth and the associated need to expand building projects. Under New Zealand law, local cities must ensure they comply with building code requirements, and Code Compliance Certificates (CCCs) must be issued within ten years. Failure to do this makes the city liable to prosecution.

The city had a large number of outstanding building compliance problems where CCCs had not been issued. Additionally, the city had already spent the fees that had been collected to do the necessary inspections on other matters.

PriorityPath® was asked to help the Resource Management Division of the Hastings City Council address and prioritize the issues and risks they were facing. The findings of the project formed the foundation for an action plan designed to reduce the council's exposure. The action plan was used to implement a successful strategy for resolving the outstanding compliance problems. The strategy also helped the staff keep inspections current and issue CCCs as local builders achieved compliance.

In compliance matters like those faced by the Hastings Council, it is important to have an overall grasp and view of all the issues and risks that need to be resolved. The rigorous nature of a PriorityPath® analysis gives the essential overview; consequently, the results lead directly to strategy development and make a major contribution toward resolving the problems that so often inhibit success.

City Planning for Wanganui

Wanganui is a city located on the beautiful east coast of New Zealand's North Island. Wanganui had recently weathered some economic difficulties—employment in the area took a hit when the government located a train repair facility outside the city. The city council had responded by encouraging expansion of the high-tech industry and trying to attract more tourists. These initiatives helped them make significant progress in overcoming their economic problems.

Considering additional steps to further improve conditions in the city, council members decided to develop a ten-year strategic development plan—then asked a world-class environmental engineering company, MWH, to work with Priority Systems® to determine the probable issues and risks they faced as they refined and implemented their plan. The mayor and city council, along with key management and staff, participated in a PriorityPath® project that assigned priorities to actions participants believed were essential to implementing the ten-year strategic development plan.

One of the findings centered on probable problems in upgrading the infrastructure for the next level of expansion. Additional potable water and upgraded water treatment facilities were needed to accommodate expected growth in population; the project helped determine a rationale that would generate support for the significant capital expenditure that would be needed to accomplish the major improvements in infrastructure that were anticipated. Their strategic development plan for the next ten years was modified to address these needs.

A ten-year plan usually represents a best-guess of the future, and it can be derailed or interrupted by new issues that always seem to arise. While all potential problems cannot be known until they actually occur, many issues/risks can be anticipated and steps can be taken to avoid their impact before they occur. Based on the identification of high-priority issues/risks, Wanganui was able to prevent many of the anticipated problems.

A Mid-Sized City Police Department

A mid-sized city police department needed to develop a corporate strategy—and we were asked to help determine the effectiveness of current programs, prioritize emergent issues, and provide the framework for generating long-range plans and policies.

Working with PriorityPath® analysts, selected stakeholders determined what needed to be accomplished. Stakeholders in the police department then identified the issues and formatted a diagram that listed everything the participants judged to be essential to accomplishing the mission successfully. The participants then determined the relative significance of each issue. These measurements enabled the officers to precisely determine the relative seriousness of each issue and group of issues. Finally, the participants examined the findings and formulated them into theme areas that allowed the police department to develop specific short-, mid-, and long-term directions.

The chief of police participated in the process and announced several initiatives that would be taken immediately, and the planning department used the findings to formulate a strategic plan. The resulting plan provided strategic direction for the police department over the next several years and became the basis on which action plans meeting the expectations of participants were built.

E. EDUCATION

Student Achievement

PriorityPath® has been used to evaluate the effectiveness of a number of school programs, primarily to improve the effectiveness of teaching and to increase student scores on standardized achievement tests. These projects included school evaluation projects with Indian Affairs in Alberta and Ontario and with public school systems in Alberta, California, Mississippi, Cleveland, Chicago, Miami, New York, and Washington, D.C. The analyses occurred within specific schools and involved interviews with administrators, supervisors, staff, parents, and board members.

In most schools, a prepared, standard database was modified to meet local conditions. This modified material was then validated by a representative sample of people associated with the school. Profiles that specified the priorities of administrators, teachers, parents, students, and the board were made available to the participants, and specific programs that addressed major needs were then generated and implemented. Participating schools saw significant improvement in student achievement on standardized tests.

A major U.S. bank funded specific projects over a five-year period in selected city schools with the objective of making improvements that would be useful in other schools across the nation. At the conclusion of this project, a number of school systems became involved in similar activities.

In one large western state, a Department of Education initiative was implemented to secure improvements in selected schools where achievement records were particularly low. Several hundred schools participated, and results in these projects were highly successful—student achievement was increased markedly in each participating school.

An interesting observation was made about needs in the many schools that participated in this program. Initially it was theorized that some common factors might provide specific clues about generic changes that needed to be made to improve scholastic records. But these expected generic solutions to sometimes common problems were not found. Although less than acceptable results were frequently found in the schools at the outset of a project, in many instances the causative factors that project participants selected as being most critical were very different.

For example, participants in one high school said that more challenging curriculum content was needed if overall student achievement was to improve. After implementing a precalculus program, student achievement generally—not only those in the precalculus courses—improved significantly. In a nearby school participants felt that a more robust sports program was an urgent need; when a successful football team was fielded and became increasingly successful, academic achievement throughout the school improved. We concluded that a major factor in improving schools is ensuring the people associated with it—including teachers, parents, students, and members of the community—feel pride in what is occurring in the school. And the source of that pride doesn't seem to matter; it may be in academic excellence, in athletic achievement, or in arts programs. The effects seem to have important ramifications for achievement in most other areas as well.

Modification of School Grant Structure

In one Canadian province, a PriorityPath® project resulted in modification of a Department of Education formula for funding rural schools. The project was an outcome of examining factors associated with providing quality education in three rural counties, where opportunities for students were becoming severely limited. All three county school systems were experiencing declining enrollments as farms were being consolidated. This led to a reduction in government grants, the amounts of which were tied to enrollments. School board access to supplementary funds was also declining. These supplementary funds were raised by a local property tax.

Resistance to increasing local property tax had increased, exacerbated by a drought that had limited farm income over several years. Residents of the counties, however, were just as interested in securing an excellent education for their students as was anyone else in the province. To conserve their resources, the county school boards had cut back services in many of the schools. The composite high schools, where innovative technical and career education programs had been proliferating, were the focus of many of these cutbacks. With loss of enrollment, there were too few students to support specialty classes. Instead, students in these schools were being offered academic courses only. Policies were reluctantly implemented that required those who wanted something other than university preparation courses to wait until they had graduated from high school before they could begin their vocational studies.

These rather severe program restrictions produced results that were unsatisfactory to the boards, the parents, and members of the communities. First, the restrictions on course offerings were causing the dropout rate to increase. Second, some parents—at their own expense—had begun to transport their students to distant urban schools where they could experience vocational, fine arts, recreational, and athletic opportunities.

The PriorityPath® projects showed that the problems in all three counties were being caused by similar factors. The boards concluded that some changes in provincial funding were needed, or the future of education in the province's rural areas would continue to be disappointing.

The three boards met with the Minister of Education. In the next session of the legislature, special funding was approved to support basic educational programs in rural schools. The boards, with the evidence provided by our analysis, were successful in stemming the movement toward reduced educational offerings for rural county children.

Amalgamation of School Boards

Long-standing animosity had existed between and among the communities in Canada's Bonnyville/Cold Lake/Grande Centre region of Northern Alberta. People in the area are a broad mixture of typical Canadians—including Indians, Métis, French Canadians, English, Ukrainian, and White Russian—complicated by a well-traveled, professional military group at the Air Force base that was recognized as being more "cosmopolitan."

Because of the potpourri of backgrounds and cultures, the makeup of the school jurisdictions in this area was an anomaly in Alberta. The original district in the area had been established under the Northwest Territories before 1890. By 1980, this original district was known as a Roman Catholic Public School District. There were three Roman Catholic Separate Districts, the Northlands School Division, the Bonnyville School Division, a public high school district, an independent district on the Cold Lake Canadian Forces

Base, and several Protestant Separate School Districts—ten solidly entrenched entities in all. Ordinarily, an area this size might have two or, at most, four school jurisdictions.

The primary intent of the Department of Education was not to bridge the differences or to change the structure of the school districts—it was to address how educational matters would be affected by construction nearby of a large new petrochemical processing plant. Numerous environmental impact studies looking at many aspects of the plant had already been conducted—but no one had considered the schools. School officials were concerned that the expected influx of population could have a disastrous impact on the education of their children, as well as the children that would move to the area. This had happened in other places in the province where rapid growth had occurred.

Priority Systems® was employed, and our analysts found information gathering to be a tense job; there was general suspicion that we had been instructed by the Department of Education to influence the outcome of the project. But surprisingly, widespread agreement occurred as participants learned that many of the issues they were concerned about had been quietly resolved years earlier. (We often find that our analysis resolves misunderstandings—and, as in this case, long-standing issues.)

Results of our project made clear that before school problems associated with construction of the new plant could be successfully addressed, there were issues about the organization of the school districts that had to be resolved. Consequently, the school boards and area residents followed up rapidly. They recognized that the long-standing competition for position and funding would not serve the needs of anyone in the community. They needed assurance that children of the additional people that would be arriving in the community would be accompanied by the funds that would be necessary to provide the education that was needed.

Public meetings were hastily called. Boards met privately. They petitioned the Minister of Education to attend a public meeting where alternatives could be examined.

Shortly after the large public meeting was held in Bonnyville, the minister received a petition from a majority of the boards urging immediate action. This was sufficient to motivate change. Rather quickly, the ten existing districts were amalgamated into four districts, an action that had appeared out of reach before we conducted the PriorityPath® project.

The cost of our project was quickly overshadowed by significant cost savings for the Department of Education and consequent tax advantages to the residents. The results were so remarkable, in fact, that the news media reported them as being a precedent in Canadian educational history. Additionally, the PriorityPath® activity was detailed in a doctoral dissertation by Robert Iles at the University of Alberta's Department of Educational Administration.

University IT Systems

PriorityPath® has also been used in several universities to determine the priority issues that needed to be addressed as new IT systems were being installed. Another consulting company with which we have been associated has been involved in launching IT systems with many universities and colleges. They have found that implementing new IT systems usually requires a detailed assessment of needs, fitting the new programs to the new circumstances and training staff in operation of the new systems. Use of PriorityPath® has reduced the time needed to launch new systems and has helped to make the new system more functional by ensuring that the unique needs of each organization are addressed and accommodated during installation of the new system.

University Student Services

PriorityPath® has also been used to assess priorities and specify needs for development and improvement of student services in two large universities.

In the first, a large university had appointed a special committee to assess and recommend directions for student services. For approximately one year, students, faculty, administration, alumni, and parents were invited to submit suggestions to the university via e-mail. The committee received approximately 6,000 submissions. Concurrently, the committee conducted approximately sixty-five focus group sessions with selected individuals from the same groups. Their final task was to assess and report the priorities of the groups so that planning for necessary changes would accommodate the judgments of users.

Techniques to accomplish the analysis were sought, both internally and from the IT company that had previously helped then install a student services IT system. The IT company referred the university to Priority Systems® because they knew the approach we use could successfully analyze the data.

The project presented some new challenges. No interviews were needed; the e-mails and focus group notes addressed every issue anyone had identified about improving student services. The special committee of the university that initiated the project had the assistance of several students to collect and organize the voluminous data. This student group worked with us, helping extract categories of concerns from the information that had been contributed.

The timeline for producing products was extremely short; a first validation of material in diagrammatic format was scheduled to occur within ten days of when we started the project. By using speech recognition software, we were able to generate crisp, focused statements of issues within the required time. After considerable editing, we produced four diagrams containing more than 1,100 items submitted by contributors. On the tenth day the charts were displayed in the university's student center, where hundreds of students examined the issues that the university community had generated. The president of the university, together with many members of the administration, faculty, and staff, also spent several hours editing, revising, and adding to the material in the diagrams. At the end of the period, we had four charts that were generally accepted by the entire university community as representing valid and diverse viewpoints for improving student services.

Nearly 700 people representing each of the participating groups rated the relative significance of the 1,100 issues. The priorities of freshmen, sophomores, juniors, seniors, graduate students, faculty, staff, administration, alumni, and parents were presented in a summary report to the special committee. The committee examined similarities and differences among the groups, noting that interests varied according to the experience and responsibility each group had for the various aspects of student services.

The special committee prepared a final report with specific recommendations for improvement that reflected the judgments of every sector within the university community. Administration received the report, thanked the committee, and implemented many aspects of their recommendations over the next few months.

A few months later, the IT organization with whom we frequently partner conducted a similar analysis of student services in a large state university on the West Coast. They integrated the student services study with implementation of a new IT program. The program was successful.

PriorityPath® was used to develop priority-critical elements for inclusion in strategic development plans in two large city school districts. Following each project, specific plans were written and implemented by school board personnel.

F. VOLUNTEER AGENCY PROJECTS

An International Relief Program

Several years ago, a large church organization arranged for excess supplies of donated wheat to be sent to areas throughout the world where hunger was prevalent. The program was extremely successful. Before long, the needs for wheat in third world countries far exceeded what church congregations could supply through personal donations. The church contacted the national agency responsible for the sale of wheat, requesting that some of the surplus supplies being stored by the agency be directed toward the international relief work the church was pursuing. The agency agreed, matched donations bushel for bushel, and arranged for the church to distribute it along with the wheat it was already sending abroad. This multiplied the effectiveness of the program substantially.

Within a short period, the efforts of the church were recognized throughout the world. Six additional churches expressed a desire to assist in this humanitarian effort. They contacted the national agency that was supplying surplus wheat, wanting to secure the same type of participation the original church had arranged. The national agency agreed, but stipulated that they would only deal with one group, suggesting that the six additional churches form a consortium with the church that originated the program and that they work together to provide even greater relief across the globe.

The consortium was formed, with the originating church taking the lead in the program they had pioneered. This arrangement continued, enjoying great success and international recognition for several years. Eventually, however, some strains in relationships among the players began to occur. Wanting to avoid confrontation, and with a strong desire to see the program continue, leaders of the originating church together with representatives of the other six churches engaged in a PriorityPath® program designed to identify, prioritize, and set the stage for resolution of the strains that had emerged.

Members of the executive committee of the consortium met and together identified the issues on which there were divergent views. A typical database was prepared, presented in cause/effect format, and results were made available to members of the consortium.

It was determined that the issues on which views had diverged could be solved. Adjustments were made, and the program for supplying wheat to impoverished areas continues.

A Volunteer Rescue Squad

For many years, volunteers living in and near a large city in the southern United States operated a rescue service that provided emergency services to people in the area surrounding the city. The service also cooperated with city emergency services to provide supplementary assistance as needed.

The rescue service was supported primarily by contributions from individuals and organizations in the community. Their reputation for excellence was appreciated locally and has been recognized nationally. Procedures they developed have been used to train emergency services personnel from all parts of the country.

Even with that recognition, the organization faced questions about its organizational structure, and it contracted with Priority Systems® to conduct an analysis of factors they were facing. Executives formed a steering committee to direct a project that would examine management practices, staffing issues, communications, training, and public relations and to explore the future of the rescue service.

We conducted interviews with a large contingent of people who were involved in and associated with the rescue service. These people identified 292 issues of significance, probing every aspect of the service that presented problems to the organization. Among the identified issues were factors relating to equipment, facilities, and other physical needs of the organization—as well as issues related to attitudes, interrelationships among members, organizational structure, and many of the human factors that are of such great consequence when the success of an organization depends on human interaction.

The results were examined by the members of the rescue service and many of the people with whom they interact. Some immediate changes were made—but the most important value to the organization was the framework it provided for planning its future.

APPENDIX E

EXECUTIVE SUMMARY, COLUMBIA ACCIDENT INVESTIGATION BOARD

Executive Summary[1]

The Columbia Accident Investigation Board's independent investigation into the February 1, 2003, loss of the Space Shuttle *Columbia* and its seven-member crew lasted nearly seven months. A staff of more than 120, along with some 400 NASA engineers, supported the Board's 13 members. Investigators examined more than 30,000 documents, conducted more than 200 formal interviews, heard testimony from dozens of expert witnesses, and reviewed more than 3,000 inputs from the general public. In addition, more than 25,000 searchers combed vast stretches of the Western United States to retrieve the spacecraft's debris. In the process, *Columbia*'s tragedy was compounded when two debris searchers with the U.S. Forest Service perished in a helicopter accident.

The Board recognized early on that the accident was probably not an anomalous, random event, but rather likely rooted to some degree in NASA's history and the human space flight program's culture. Accordingly, the Board broadened its mandate at the outset to include an investigation of a wide range of historical and organizational issues, including political and budgetary considerations, compromises, and changing priorities over the life of the Space Shuttle Program. The Board's conviction regarding the importance of these factors strengthened as the investigation progressed, with the result that this report, in its findings, conclusions, and recommendations, places as much weight on these causal factors as on the more easily understood and corrected physical cause of the accident.

The physical cause of the loss of *Columbia* and its crew was a breach in the Thermal Protection System on the leading edge of the left

---

[1] Columbia Accident Investigation Board, *Report Volume 1*, August 2003, Washington, D.C.: Government Printing Office.

wing, caused by a piece of insulating foam which separated from the left bipod ramp section of the External Tank at 81.7 seconds after launch, and struck the wing in the vicinity of the lower half of Reinforced Carbon-Carbon panel number 8. During reentry this breach in the Thermal Protection System allowed superheated air to penetrate through the leading edge insulation and progressively melt the aluminum structure of the left wing, resulting in a weakening of the structure until increasing aerodynamic forces caused loss of control, failure of the wing, and break-up of the Orbiter. This breakup occurred in a flight regime in which, given the current design of the Orbiter, there was no possibility for the crew to survive.

The organizational causes of this accident are rooted in the Space Shuttle Program's history and culture, including the original compromises that were required to gain approval for the Shuttle, subsequent years of resource constraints, fluctuating priorities, schedule pressures, mischaracterization of the Shuttle as operational rather than developmental, and lack of an agreed national vision for human space flight. Cultural traits and organizational practices detrimental to safety were allowed to develop, including: reliance on past success as a substitute for sound engineering practices (such as testing to understand why systems were not performing in accordance with requirements); organizational barriers that prevented effective communication of critical safety information and stifled professional differences of opinion; lack of integrated management across program elements; and the evolution of an informal chain of command and decision-making processes that operated outside the organization's rules.

This report discusses the attributes of an organization that could more safely and reliably operate the inherently risky Space Shuttle, but does not provide a detailed organizational prescription. Among those attributes are: a robust and independent program technical authority that has complete control over specifications and requirements, and waivers to them; an independent safety assurance organization with line authority over all levels of safety oversight; and an organizational culture that reflects the best characteristics of a learning organization.

This report concludes with recommendations, some of which are specifically identified and prefaced as "before return to flight." These recommendations are largely related to the physical cause of the accident, and include preventing the loss of foam, improved imaging of the Space Shuttle stack from liftoff through separation of the External Tank, and on-orbit inspection and repair of the Thermal Protection System. The remaining recommendations, for the most part, stem from the Board's findings on organizational cause factors. While they are not "before return to flight" recommendations, they can be viewed as "continuing to fly" recommendations, as they capture the Board's thinking on what changes are necessary to operate the Shuttle and future spacecraft safely in the mid to long-term.

These recommendations reflect the board's strong support for return to flight at the earliest date consistent with the overriding objective of the study, and its conviction that operation of the space shuttle—and all human space flight—is a developmental activity with high inherent risks.

APPENDIX F

EXAMPLE PRIORITYPATH® CHART

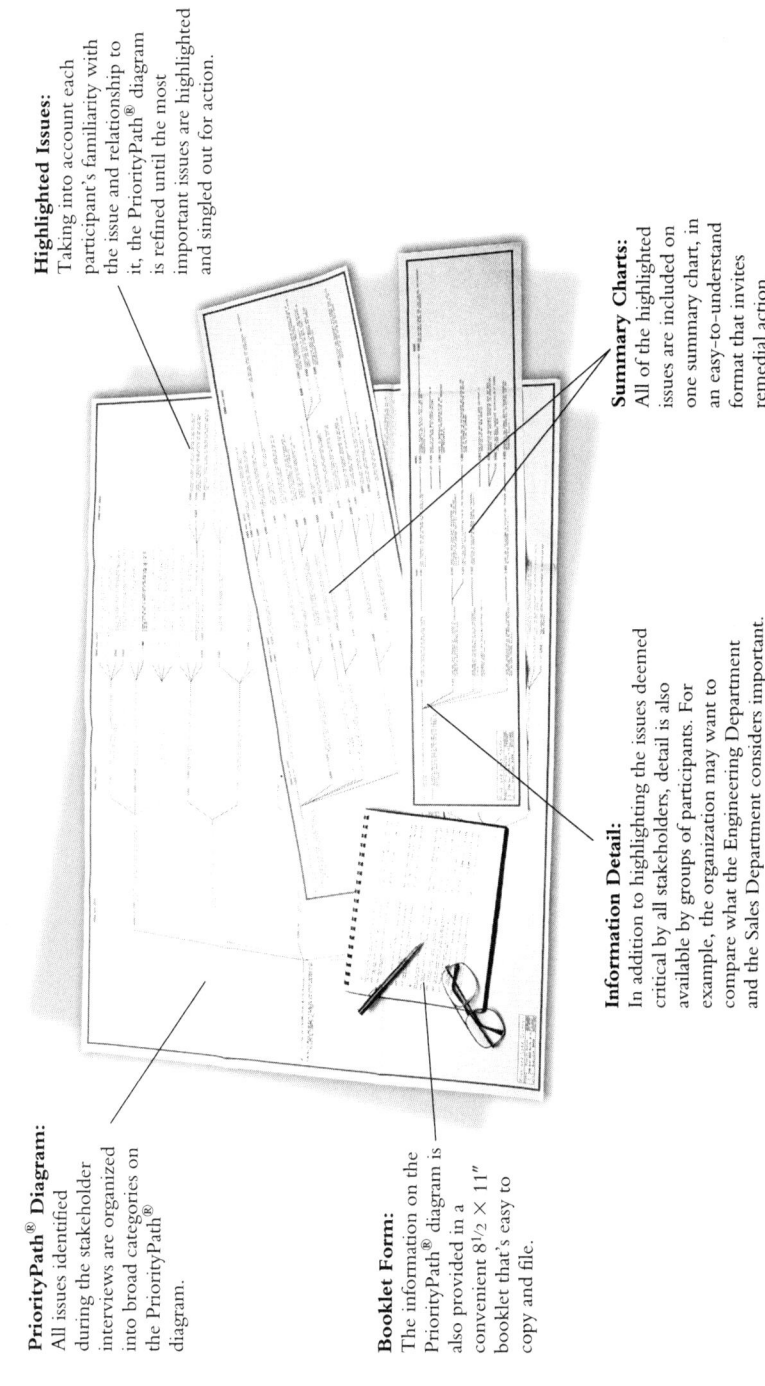

PriorityPath® Diagram:
All issues identified during the stakeholder interviews are organized into broad categories on the PriorityPath® diagram.

Booklet Form:
The information on the PriorityPath® diagram is also provided in a convenient 8½ × 11" booklet that's easy to copy and file.

Information Detail:
In addition to highlighting the issues deemed critical by all stakeholders, detail is also available by groups of participants. For example, the organization may want to compare what the Engineering Department and the Sales Department considers important.

Highlighted Issues:
Taking into account each participant's familiarity with the issue and relationship to it, the PriorityPath® diagram is refined until the most important issues are highlighted and singled out for action.

Summary Charts:
All of the highlighted issues are included on one summary chart, in an easy-to-understand format that invites remedial action.

REFERENCES RELATED TO TEAM ACTIVITY CONSULTED: FURTHER READING

1. Aguayo, Rafael. *Dr. Deming: The American Who Taught the Japanese About Quality.* New York: Simon and Schuster, 1990.
2. Cormack, David. *Team Spirit.* Grand Rapids, Michigan: Pyranee Books, Zondervan Publishing House, 1989.
3. Crosby, Philip B. *Quality is Free: The Art of Making Quality Certain.* New York: McGraw-Hill, 1979.
4. Crosby, Philip B. *Quality Without Tears: The Art of Hassle-Free Management.* New York: McGraw-Hill, 1984.
5. Dobyns, Lloyd, and Crawford-Mason, Clare. *Quality or Else: The Revolution in World Business.* Boston: Houghton Mifflin, 1991.
6. Fisher, Kimball. *Leading Self-Directed Work Teams.* New York: McGraw-Hill, 1993.
7. Hart, W.L., and Bogan, Christopher E. *The Baldrige: What It is, How It's Won, How to Use It to Improve Quality in Your Company.* New York: McGraw-Hill, 1992.
8. Katzenback, Jon R., and Smith, Douglas K. *The Wisdom of Teams.* Boston: Harvard Business School Press, 1993.
9. Scholtes, Peter, et al. *The Team Handbook.* Madison: Joiner, 1991.
10. Scott, Cynthia D, and Jaffe, Dennis T. *Empowerment: A Practical Guide for Success.* Los Altos, California: Crisp Publications, 1991.
11. Townsend, Patrick L. *Commit to Quality.* New York: Wiley, 1990.
12. Townsend, Patrick L. *Quality in Action.* New York: Wiley, 1992.
13. Walton, Mary. *The Deming Management Method.* New York: Perigee, 1986.
14. Walton, Mary. *Deming Management at Work.* New York: Perigee, 1991.

INDEX

Note: Page numbers in *italic* type indicate figures.

abacus, 87
Abacus Version, 87–93
  action plan, 93
  buy-in, 88
  cause-effect diagram, 90–91
  mission statement preparation, 88
  outline, 87
  participant selection, 89–90
  project leader, 88
  review of information, 91
  sample project, 93
  steering committee, 89–90
  weighting issues, 91–92
ABC Sports, 126
actions, 50–51, 92, 94–104
  linking pins, 96
  major themes, 94–95
  recommendations format, 103–104
  recommendations process, 101–103
  remediation teams, 95–96
  team management, 96–100
  theme teams, 95–96, 100–101
airlines, 116–117
airport safety and security, 151–152
Alberta, Canada
  Energy Resources Conservation Board (ERCB), 146–149
  Environment Department, 156
  school board amalgamation, 169–171
algorithms, 30
alignment findings, 94
AltaGas, 110
"and" logic
  convergent thinking, 62–64
  example of, 59
  full speed ahead, 62, 64
  "or" logic in relation to, 63–66
  planning for success, 60–64
  predominance of, 59
arithmetic mean, 38
Army Space Initiative Study (ASIS), 132–133
assessment, 10, 19, 29, 32, 41, 51, 67
assumptions, 20
Australia
  power transmission, 127–128
  Sydney Water Board, 79–81
average, 38

Basslink, 128
battle plans, 130–131
Bay of Fundy, 150–151

beliefs, 20
bias, in survey research, 10, 37
Bloomer, Jeff, 110
Boeing, 4–5
Boulle, Pierre, 28
The Bridge on the River Kwai (Boulle), 28
Brigham Young University, 110
British Military Academy, Sandhurst, England, 25
Burnside, Ambrose P., 64–66
Burnside Bridge, 64–66
buy-in, 75, 88, *see also* involvement of people; ownership

Calgary, Canada, 109
  emergency response plan modification, 149
  Olympic Games, 125–126
Canada, *see also* Alberta, Canada; Calgary, Canada
  G8 Summit, 69–71
  power generation company, 120–121
  provincial strategic planning, 74–75
Canadian Food Grains Bank, 109
capital investment project, 129–130
cause/effect diagram, 44–45, 51, 90–91
celebration, 100
central tendency, 38
Challenger space shuttle, 5–6
champion, 34
chemical and fertilizer company, 119–120
Churchill, Winston, 25–26
city planning, 166
Civil War, 64–66
clients
  comments by, 109–110
  partial list, 111–114
  project summaries, 115–174
Columbia space shuttle disaster, 6, 175–177
commercial project summaries, 116–130
  airlines, 116–117
  Calgary Olympic Games, 125–126
  capital investment, 129–130
  chemical and fertilizer manufacturing, 119–120
  consulting practice, 124–125
  gas gathering and processing installation, 128–129
  hazardous waste facilities, 121–123
  information and communication services, 123–124

183

commercial project summaries (*continued*)
  medical services, 126–127
  power generation company, 120–121
  power transmission, 127–128
  rubber reclamation plant, 121–122
  water management, 117–119
communication
  barriers, 14–15
  knowledge versus beliefs, 20
  mid-management, 15
  openness, 15–16
  policy, 34
  system improvement and, 100
communication services, 123–124
competencies, 20–21
conflict, 17
consensus, 101
consulting, 9, 18–19, 45
consulting company, 124–125
convergent thinking, 62–64
corporate culture, 15–16, 73–74, 159, 176
counterintuition, 56
Covey, Stephen R., 54
creativity, 21
culture, organizational, 15–16, 73–74, 159, 176

daily meetings, 15–16, 116–117
data analysis and presentation, 47–52, *49*
data buckets, 90
database, 10
Decision Center, 24
Deep Battle, 130–131
Delphi Studies, 40
deviation, 38
diagnosis, 9
direct findings, 94
disaster
  confronting, 3–4
  human factors, 4–7
distribution statistics, 37–38
divergent thinking
  opposition to, 57–58
  "or" logic, 62–64
driving forces
  "and" logic, 61
  definition, 53
  preoccupation with, 54–55
  resisting forces in relation to, 54

education project summaries, 167–172
  school board amalgamation, 169–171
  school funding, 168–169
  student achievement, 167–168
  student services, 171–172
electricity market, 71–73
electronics manufacturing, 75–77
employees
  competencies, 20–21
  involvement, 35
  mismatches with supervisors, 18, 92
  motivation for giving/withholding information, 13, 17–18, 68
  respect, 99
  sources of information, 12–13, 17–19, 21, 97, 131
energy services, 73–74
EnSource Industries, 110
environmental department, 156
equilibrium, 53
ERCB, *see* Energy Resources Conservation Board (ERCB), Alberta, Canada
Esso Resources, 30–31
executives
  information lacking by, 12–13, 20–21
  mismatches with employees, 18, 92
  overconfidence, 16
  priorities, 14
  PriorityPath® effective for, 41–42
experts
  Delphi Studies, 40
  internal versus external, 18–19, 99

failure/success relation, 58–66
Farragut, David G., 3, 64, 83
Fault Tree Analysis, 47
focus, 18, 28
follow-through, 32
Foothills Operations for Shell Canada, 109
Force Field Analysis, 47, 53–54, *55*
"full speed ahead" approach, 3, 62, 64, 83
funding, 97

G8 Summit, Canada, 69–71
gas gathering and processing installation, 128–129
General Dynamics, xix
general versus specific factors, 63, 168
Gisbourne District Council, 164–165
government and regulatory agency project summaries, 150–167
  airport safety and security, 151–152
  city planning, 166
  department of environment, 156
  department of justice, 157
  Gisbourne District Council, 164–165
  Hastings City Council, 165
  housing authority, 161–163
  industrial safety, 159–161
  OH&S services, 153
  police department, 166–167
  recreation and parks departments, 153–155
  shared services project, 157–158
  Tauranga District Council, 163–164
  traffic management, 150–151
  wildlife management, 155–156
  workers' compensation board, 152–153
gratitude, 100
groups, 24, 89

Index 185

Hanson, Rick, 110
Harder, J.D., 109
Hastings City Council, 165
hazardous waste facilities, 121–123
Hewitt Oil, 148–149
hierarchical structures, 24
high-priority issues, 50–51
Hill, A.P., 65–66
Holden, Gary, 110
Honeywell, 139
Hong Kong tunnel construction, 81–82
hospital safety, 159–160
housing authority, 161–163
human factors
 analysis of, 4–7, 29, 42, 67
 Challenger space shuttle, 5–6
 mathematical models, 58
 Minuteman missile, 4–5
 operational capacity and, 135
 subjectivity, 4–7, 29–30
 terrorism, 6–7

ideal versus real, *26*, 26–27
IFR, 110
Imperial Oil, xix
implied findings, 94
indirect findings, 94
industrial safety, 159–161
information, *see also* knowledge management
 gathering, 43–44, 89–90
 managers, 17–18
 motivation for giving/withholding, 13, 17–18, 68
 outside analysts for gathering, 44
 participant review, 44–45, 91
 sources of organizational, 12–13, 18–19, 21, 97, 131
 three questions to uncover, 13, 43–44, 89
information and communication services, 123–124
international relief program, 173
interviews, 43–45
involvement of people, 35, 87–88,
 see also buy-in

justice department, 157

Kingsley, John, 109
knowledge, and power, 24–25
knowledge management, 20, *see also* information
Kramer, Gary L., 110
kurtosis, 38

Lee, Robert E., 64
Lewin, Kurt, 53
linking pins, 96
Lloyds of London, 141

M1A1 Abrams Tank, 131–132
major themes, 94–95

majority rule, 101
managers, *see also* mid-management
 mismatches with employees, 18, 92
 sources of knowledge, 17–18
 training, 99
manufacturing
 chemical and fertilizer, 119–120
 electronics, 75–77
 test instrument, 77–79
Mathematica, 30
Mayfield, David, 109
measures of shape, 38
measures of variation, 38
median, 38
medical services, 126–127
megaprojects, 141
metrics, 35
mid-management, *see also* managers
 communication barriers, 15
 training, 99
military and space project summaries, 130–134
 Army Space Initiative Study (ASIS), 132–133
 Deep Battle plans, 130–131
 M1A1 Abrams Tank, 131–132
 New Zealand Defense Forces, 133–134
military appreciation, 25–26
mining safety, 159
Minuteman missile, 4
mission statement, 43, 88
mode, 38
Montgomery Watson Harza (MWH), 79–82, 166

narrative reports, 52
NASA, 5, 175
New Zealand
 Defense Forces, 133–134
 Gisbourne District Council, 164–165
 Hastings City Council, 165
 privatization in, 71–73
 Tauranga District Council, 163–164
 Wanganui city planning, 166
nonthreatening environment for information exchange, 13, 17–18, 68
North Africa, 128–129
Nuclear Utilities Service Corporation, 31

Occupational Health and Safety, 153, 159–161
Olympic Games, Calgary, 125–126
Operations Research, xix
"or" logic
 "and" logic in relation to, 63–66
 effectiveness, 60
 example of, 60
 failure reduction, 61–62
organizations
 beliefs and assumptions, 20
 clarification of problems, 83
 culture, 15–16, 73–74, 159, 176

186   Index

organizations (*continued*)
  dynamics, 23
  interests of individuals versus, 23–24
  social systems, 23–25
  structure of, 16–17, 24, 123–124
  uniqueness of, 14
  values, 19
ownership, 9, 96, *see also* buy-in

Pareto charts, 47
Pareto principle, 48
participants in Abacus Version project, 89
Pears, Les, 109
performance assessment, *see* assessment
petrochemical industry project summaries, 134–150
  Alberta Energy Resources Conservation Board projects, 146–149
  caisson recovery problem, 144–145
  coker operational capacity, 134–135
  computer control system, 139–140
  dyke stabilization, 142
  environmental controls, 138–139
  equipment startup, 137
  expansion plant startup, 140–141
  loss management, 141, 143
  offshore drilling, 149–150
  project management priorities, 137–138
  property services, 145
  safety, 142, 143, 160–161
  sour gas management, 135–137, 142–143, 146–147
  turbine repair and operation, 143–144
Philips BTS, 109
planning, 21, 27, 27–28
  "and" logic, 59–64
  buy-in, 75
  Canadian provincial, 74–75
  "or" logic, 60–64
  system improvement and, 98
plateaus, *22*, 22–23
police department, 166–167
power, and knowledge, 24–25
power generation company, 120–121
Power Principle, 24
power transmission, 127–128
presentation of results, 47–52
Presentation of results, *49*
PriorityPath®, *see also* Abacus Version
  action determination and implementation, 50–51
  analyst role, 44, 45, 83
  beneficiaries, 41–42, 67–82, 115–174
  benefits, 33–34
  chart example, *179*
  client comments, 109–110
  client list, 111–114
  commercial project summaries, 116–130
  completeness, 10, 40
  consulting versus, 9, 18–19, 45

data analysis and presentation, 47–52, *49*
definition, 8, 29
deliverables, 51–52
Delphi Studies versus, 40
education project summaries, 167–172
effective uses, 41–42, 67–82, 115–174
exhaustiveness, 10, 40
government and regulatory agency project summaries, 150–167
information gathering, 43–44
military and space project summaries, 130–134
mission statement preparation, 43
petrochemical industry project summaries, 134–150
preparation for, 34–35
process, 42–50
project initiation with, 83–84
rating of issues, *46*, 46–48, 50, 107–108, *108*
situations ripe for, 41–42, 67–68
speed, 41
strengths, 31–33
survey research versus, 10, 36–40, *37*
traditional approaches versus, 36–40
Validation Diagram, 44–45, 51
volunteer agency project summaries, 173–174
privatization of electricity market, 71–73
probabilities, objective and subjective mixture of, 5
problem solving, 15–16, 25–26
project leaders, 88
promotions, 15

quantification/rating instrument, *46*, 51

Rand Corporation, 140–141
range, 38
rating instrument, *46*, 51
rating of issues, *46*, 46–48, 50
  Abacus Version, 91–92
  criteria, *108*
  instructions, 107–108
  real versus ideal, *26*, 26–27
  recognition, 100
recommendations
  format, 103–104
  process, 101–103
recreation and parks departments, 153–155
Rehill, David H., 109
reliability and risk equation, 58–66
remediation, 50–51, 92, 95–96
report documents, 51
rescue squad, 174
resident wisdom, 12–13
resisting forces
  definition, 53
  driving forces in relation to, 54
  measurement, 55–56
  "or" logic, 61–62

results presentation, 47–52, *49*
reviews
  information, 44–45, 91
  organizational, 35
rewards, 35
risk analysis, 36, *see also* reliability and risk equation
risk management, 8, 29–30, 32
risks, 31
rubber reclamation plant, 121–122
Rumson Corporation, xix

scalar magnitude, 38
school board amalgamation, 169–171
school funding, 168–169
Schwarzkopf, H. Norman, 131
security planning, 69–71
Senge, Peter, 53–54, 56
SEVs, *see* Strategic Event Values
Shell Canada, 109
skew, 38
specific versus general factors, 63, 168
standard deviation, 38
Stanford Research Institute, 31
statistical techniques, 37–39
  distribution statistics, 37–38
  measures of shape, 38
  measures of variation, 38
steering committees, 89–90, 95
Stephens, G.W., 109
Strategic Event Values (SEVs), 47, 48, 50–52, 94
strategic path diagrams, 52
strategic planning, *see* planning
student achievement, 167–168
student services, 171–172
success/failure relation, 58–66
Summit of the Americas, 69
survey research, 10, 36–40
Sydney Water Board, Australia, 79–81
Syncrude Consortium, 31
system improvement, 95–96, 98

Tasmania, 127–128
Tauranga District Council, 163–164
team approach, foundation of, 97

team management, 96–100
  commitment of key personnel, 97
  commitment of remediation team, 98
  communication, 100
  focus on system improvement, 98
  recognition, gratitude, celebration, 100
  training, 99
  unified plan, 98
telecommunications company, 124
terrorism, 6–7
test instrument manufacturing, 77–79
theme teams, 95–96, *96*, 100–101
themes, 94–95
Thompson, John A., 109
Total Loss Management Program, 140
TRADOC, *see* U.S. Army Training and Doctrine Command
traffic management, 150–151
training, 35, 99
trust, 32–33

U.S. Army Training and Doctrine Command (TRADOC), xix–xx
U.S. Bureau of Indian Affairs, 31
U.S. Department of Energy, Office of Integrated Risk Management, 32
U.S. Veterans Administration, 31

Validation Diagram, 44–45, 51
validation of methodology, 30–31
values, 19
variance, 38
Vector Research, xix
volunteer agency project summaries
  international relief, 173
  rescue squad, 174

Wanganui city planning, 166
water management projects, 79–81, 117–119, 163–164
Welch, John R., Jr., 99
Wholesale Electricity Market Development Group (WEMDG), 71–73
wildlife management, 155–156
Wolfram Research, 30
workers' compensation board, 152–153
World Trade Organization (WTO), 69

About TEXERE

Texere, a progressive and authoritative voice in business publishing, brings to the global business community the expertise and insights of leading thinkers. Our books educate, enlighten, and entertain, and provide an intersection where our authors and our readers share cutting edge ideas, practices, and innovative solutions. Texere seeks to cultivate, enhance, and disseminate information that illuminates the global business landscape.

www.thomson.com/learning/texere

About the typeface

This book was set in 10.5/14pt Bembo. Bembo was cut by Francesco Griffo for the Venitian printer Aldus Manutius to publish in 1495 *De Aetna* by Cardinal Pietro Bembo. Stanley Morison supervised the design of Bembo for the Monotype Corporation in 1929. The Bembo is a readable and classical typeface because of its well-proportioned letterforms, functional serifs, and lack of peculiarities.

Library of Congress Cataloging-in-Publication Data

Stringham, Bryant L.
   Finding the priority path : overcoming organizational obstacles / Bryant L. Stringham, Jon D. Stephens; in conjunction with Interlink Capital Strategies with contributions from Alan J. Beard.
   p. cm.
   ISBN 0-324-31219-9
   1. Organizational behavior.   2. Organizational effectiveness.
   3. Corporate culture.   I. Stephens, Jon D.   II. Title.
   HD58.7.S77 2005
   658.4'013—dc22

2005022119